TODAY
ROBERT HOLMAN

A Methuen New Theatrescript
Methuen · London and New York

To Paul and Natasha Copley

Front cover photograph: David Seymour

A METHUEN PAPERBACK

First published in Great Britain as a Methuen Paperback original in 1985 by Methuen London Ltd, 11 New Fetter Lane, London EC4P 4EE and in the United States of America by Methuen Inc, 733 Third Avenue, New York, NY 10017

Copyright © 1985 by Robert Holman
Music for all the songs, except 'Lord Byron' (which is a traditional tune) copyright © 1985 by Richard Springate
Lyrics to 'Lord Byron' copyright © 1985 by Martin Carthy

Holman, Robert, *1952-*
    Today.
    I. Title
    822'.914   PR6058.04535
    ISBN 0-413-59490-4

CAUTION
This play is fully protected by copyright. All rights are reserved and all enquiries concerning the rights for professional or amateur stage productions should be made to Margaret Ramsay Ltd, 14a Goodwin's Court, St Martin's Lane, London WC2N 4LL.

Introduction

In 1983 the RSC asked me if I would like to write a play for a section of the acting company who would be resident in Stratford-upon-Avon the following year. The play published here is the result of that collaboration, and it was felt that some readers might be interested to know a little of the background to the writing of it.

    Normally a play is written, and then cast. With *Today* the reverse is true. I met the director, Bill Alexander, early in 1984 and he told me the actors who would be in my play. There were thirteen. A few I knew very briefly because they had been on the previous year's small scale tour, playing two Shakespeare plays, and the rest I didn't know at all. In March I went to Stratford to meet them properly. I know we were all nervous: they had committed themselves to an unwritten script with no guarantee of the type of part they might play, and I hadn't a clue what I was going to write about. During the next six weeks we spent as much time together as their hectic timetables allowed. I went into rehearsals for their other productions. We met in the pub, often late at night after performances. We ate and played 'Trivial Pursuit' together in the greenroom. We rowed on the Avon, and a few of us even went to the circus. It was a way of getting to know them socially, without pressure or expectation: I wasn't there to delve into their private worlds, but wanted to know them as actors. At the end of this period Bill Alexander suggested I write a series of short duologues, which he then directed them in. I wrote the duologues quickly, more or less off the top of my head, but they were a way of seeing what I might eventually be able to write for them, and it gave them the chance to see my work.

    In the middle of May I left Stratford, still with no idea of what I was going to write about, but a clear idea of who I was writing it for. The interwar years and the Spanish Civil War have always interested me, so I ended up writing about that. In September I returned to Stratford with a script and we began rehearsing. The play opened at The Other Place in October.

    The brief from the RSC had been to write my own play, and to use the actors' talents as best I could. I make no claim to being completely successful in this, but what I do know is that the play published here would not have been the same without them. *Today* is a tribute to their dedication, energy and enthusiasm.

Robert Holman
February 1985

Today was first performed by the Royal Shakespeare Company at The Other Place, Stratford-upon-Avon, on 23 October 1984, with the following cast:

PEGGY SMITH	Penny Downie
VICTOR ELLISON	Roger Allam
RICHARD HURLL	David Whitaker
THOMAS ELLISON	George Raistrick
LUCY ELLISON	Amanda Root
WILFRED FOX	Jimmy Yuill
DOROTHY ELLISON	Rowena Roberts
CONSTABLE PRICE	Donald McKillop
REBECCA ELLISON	Kelly Gregory/Charlotte Williams
EDWARD LONGRESSE	James Simmons
ELIZABETH BRADLEY	Polly James
ERNEST HURLL	David Whitaker
HEINZ BAYER	Simon Templeman
PETER DEAN	Jim Hooper
SISTER MARY-JOSEPH	Katharine Rogers

MUSICIANS: Charles Duncan (piano/drum); Ian Reynolds (flute/alto flute/piccolo); Richard Springate (violin/viola/mandolin)

Directed by Bill Alexander
Set designed by William Dudley
Costumes designed by Allan Watkins
Lighting by Wayne Dowdeswell
Music arranged and researched by Martin Carthy and Richard Springate
Sound by John A Leonard
Stage Manager Richard Oriel
Deputy Stage Manager Simon Dodson
Assistant Stage Manager Kate Trevers

ACT ONE	ACT TWO
1936	1937
1920	1946
1923	

A Note on the Music

The play is partly about a composer and music played an integral part in the original production. The bare bones of the music and the words, where indicated in the text, have been included at the end of this volume. Music was also used during the scene changes, at first very simply, but slowly becoming more complicated and symphonic in character as the play progressed. The music Victor dictates in Act Two, Scene Four is the folk tune, found by Martin Carthy, upon which all the music was based.

A Note on the Calendar

For the original production William Dudley designed a wooden calendar which stood at the back of the set and showed the date of each scene. It worked brilliantly.

ACT ONE

In the half-light, the Company sing the folk tune on which VICTOR *will base his piece of music.*

Scene One

The lights are snapped up.
A secluded place on the vast lawns of Guisborough Priory.
Monday October 5th, 1936.
The sky is overcast and full of cloud.
On the grass there is a small wicker basket. The handle of an umbrella protrudes from it.
PEGGY SMITH *is standing near the basket. It also contains her purse and a few personal things.*
PEGGY *was born in 1908. She is a well-heeled woman with a fine bone structure. Her face is bright and alert. She is wearing an autumn coat with a matching hat.*
VICTOR ELLISON *is standing near her.*
VICTOR *was born in 1902. He is a big, squarely-built man with thick black hair. He is wearing a good, nut-brown suit which is chalk marked from a school classroom. He has chalk on the ends of his fingers and a yellow nicotine stain.*
VICTOR *is bent almost double, breathing deeply. He has just entered. He has his hat in his hand.*

VICTOR: I'm sorry. Rebecca's had an accident. I've been at the hospital most of the morning.

PEGGY (*gently, concerned*): Don't worry, what's she done.

VICTOR: Only cut her finger, the little fool.

PEGGY: Victor –

VICTOR: I was more sympathetic with her. (*Showing* PEGGY *the side of his left index finger.*) Here.

PEGGY: How?

VICTOR: On some plateglass.

PEGGY: At school?

VICTOR: Yes. One of the little boys was larking about. On a door. He pushed her into it. She put her hand out to steady herself.

PEGGY: Poor Beccy.

VICTOR: Her headmistress telephoned me. I've so much on, what with the Christmas concert and everything.

PEGGY: Have they stitched it?

VICTOR: No. It's worse than that, unfortunately. That's why I'm in a state.

PEGGY: Which doctor saw her?

VICTOR: A junior doctor. Then your father.

PEGGY *is looking at* VICTOR.
There is a moment's silence.

Yes, that's what I thought.

PEGGY: You didn't say anything?

VICTOR: Yes, Peggy, I told him all about us.

A slight pause.

PEGGY: Poor you.

VICTOR: I expect it's one of those things.

VICTOR *holds out his hand.* PEGGY *takes it; their hands fumble together.* VICTOR *straightens up.*

PEGGY: She needs surgery?

VICTOR: Mmm. (*Brightly.*) Well, Dr Smith?

PEGGY: It's not my field, Victor. He's good. I should trust him.

They are holding hands. PEGGY *points to the side of her own left index finger.*

Here? What's Daddy said?

VICTOR: As little as possible.

PEGGY: She's severed the tendon?

VICTOR: Yes. Is it serious, or very serious?

PEGGY: Quite serious.

A slight pause.

Would you like me to be at the hospital?

VICTOR: I don't see how we can. When I took her in I was praying you'd be there.

PEGGY: Didn't you know I wouldn't be?

VICTOR (*brightly*): Yes.

PEGGY (*after a moment's pause*): I'd have to wander in unbeknown. What time's he operating?

VICTOR: This afternoon. I don't even know what he's going t'do.

PEGGY: Try and find the two ends of the tendon and stitch them back. They're difficult things. (*Pointing to the top of his palm.*) It's most likely that the free end will have sprung up here. The first thing he'll have to do is to find it – it'll be lying somewhere in the soft tissue of the palm.

PEGGY *looks at him.*

VICTOR: Go on.

PEGGY: That means opening up the length of her finger until he comes across it.

VICTOR: Is it as vague as that?

PEGGY: Yes.

PEGGY *hesitates.*

VICTOR: You were going to say something else?

PEGGY: The pattern of the suture he'll use to re-attach the tendon is very complicated.

VICTOR: I thought you said it wasn't your field.

PEGGY: It isn't.

VICTOR: Go on.

PEGGY: I live with Daddy – we obviously talk with one another.

VICTOR (*leaning forward*): Stop hiding, Peggy.

PEGGY (*looking at him*): Am I?

Their hands fumble together. They kiss each other. They embrace in a longer kiss.

VICTOR: Is it a new operation?

PEGGY: Yes, quite new. He'll be keen to do it.

VICTOR: That makes sense.

PEGGY: It's an operation pioneered in America. He's been waiting. The best results have been obtained with children.

VICTOR: How good a surgeon is he?

PEGGY: Brilliant.

They kiss.
A slight pause.
Their lips move apart.
A slight pause.
Their hands fumble together.

Especially with hands. He's a genius.

VICTOR (*smiling*): He skipped around like a spring lamb. I think he thought it was Christmas.

PEGGY: I could wander in.

VICTOR: Not you as well.

PEGGY *frees her hand. She walks away a pace.*

(*Stepping behind her, putting his arms round her waist:*) I'm sorry.

PEGGY: Yes, that was very unfair.

PEGGY *turns round. They rub noses.*

VICTOR: I want to make love to you.

PEGGY: I want to make love to you.

RICHARD HURLL *enters.*
RICHARD *was born in 1910. He is a small, squat, broad-shouldered man with sunken eyes. He seems to be wearing all the old clothes he possesses. There is an old rucksack on his back and thick walking boots on his feet.*
VICTOR *and* PEGGY *move apart slightly.*

RICHARD: Could yer tell us the way to Whitby, please?

VICTOR: Er – which road d'you want?

RICHARD: That's what I thought I was askin' you like?

VICTOR: If you go out of the priory. Turn left. Follow the road down t'the market cross. Turn left again. Yer'll be on it.

RICHARD: Left. The market cross. Turn left.

VICTOR: There is another road, depending which you want?

RICHARD: I'm after gettin' t'Whitby. The quickest, yer know.

PEGGY: Are you on foot?

RICHARD: Aye.

PEGGY: I can give you a lift part of the way. (*To* VICTOR:) Am I going to the hospital?

VICTOR (*surprised; it takes him a second to think*): No.

PEGGY: I can take you to the Castleton turn off.

ACT ONE

RICHARD: That'd be great like if yer could.

PEGGY: There's a Riley parked by the church. It is open.

RICHARD: Aye.

A slight pause.

Where's the church like?

RICHARD: Turn right instead of left. It's facing you. Sit inside.

RICHARD: 'A will. Ta very much.

PEGGY: I might be a few minutes.

RICHARD: You take yer time like.

RICHARD *goes.*

VICTOR: Where the hell did he come from?

PEGGY (*walking away a pace*): I don't know.

VICTOR: I think I ate my heart. Where are you going?

PEGGY: I thought I might go to an auction this afternoon, at Danby. There was some particularly nice silver in the catalogue. Daddy wants me to bid for some cutlery.

VICTOR *is looking at her.*

VICTOR: This can't go on, can it?

PEGGY: Why not? I'm happy.

VICTOR: Are you?

PEGGY *is looking at him.*

PEGGY: I'd hate to lose you, Victor.

VICTOR: Me, too.

There is a moment's silence between them.
VICTOR *holds out his hand, their hands fumble together.*

The operation will be safe, won't it?

PEGGY: He wouldn't do it if it wasn't.

VICTOR: I was meaning the anaesthetic.

PEGGY (*smiling*): I know.

VICTOR: It seems a dangerous event for one little finger.

PEGGY: Stop worrying.

It starts to rain. It happens suddenly. It is raining hard.

(*Going to her basket:*) I've got an umbrella.

PEGGY *puts it up. They stand beneath it.*

VICTOR (*smiling*): Thank goodness for you.

PEGGY (*smiling*): Thank goodness for me.

VICTOR (*taking her hand*): I love you, Peggy.

There is a moment's silence between them.

It hasn't sunk in yet about Beccy.

PEGGY: That's quite usual.

VICTOR: Is it? I hope I've done the right thing. The decision to go ahead didn't seem to involve me.

PEGGY: Trust him. Have faith.

VICTOR: I find having faith very difficult. I never used to. It's age.

PEGGY *smiles.*

What're you smiling at?

PEGGY: Worrier.

VICTOR (*smiling*): Give over, woman.

PEGGY: I'd feel out of place pushed in front of a class of rowdy schoolboys.

VICTOR: They're not rowdy in my class.

PEGGY (*a twinkle in her eye*): Are you harsh with them?

VICTOR: Firm.

PEGGY *moves to kiss him.*

Today we're specialists, aren't we?

PEGGY: What?

VICTOR: Specialist knowledge. Today there's so much it would take a lifetime to begin to understand.

PEGGY *puts her free hand inside his jacket, round his waist.*

We have to begin to accept and not question.

PEGGY: What are you talking about?

VICTOR: Helplessness. (*Smiling.*) Ignore me.

PEGGY: I don't want to ignore you.

VICTOR: I feel happier ignored.

PEGGY: Victor.

VICTOR: No, I do.

PEGGY: Why?

VICTOR: That's not the complete truth.

PEGGY: Nothing ever is.

VICTOR: No.

The church clock nearby begins its chime, ready to strike the hour.

Is it two o'clock already?

PEGGY: Yes.

A slight pause.

If ever you want anything, you know I'm here.

VICTOR: Thanks, love.

PEGGY: D'you mean it?

VICTOR (*looking at her*): Of course I do.

They kiss.
The clock strikes.

I'd better go and teach those boys some music.

VICTOR *exits towards the school.*
The sky has become very dark.
Sudden blackout.

Scene Two

The lights are snapped up.
The moors a few miles from Guisborough. Beside the grassy verge of the Whitby road is a dry-stone wall which has fallen down in the middle.
Two hours later. Four o'clock.
It has stopped raining. The sky is brighter. There is a rainbow.
THOMAS ELLISON is repairing the wall with a stonemason's hammer. He works methodically, slowly, reshaping the stones, and then fitting them back.
THOMAS's jacket is resting on top of the wall. His bicycle is leaning against it. The bicycle is a travelling tool kit. Fastened to it in all sorts of ingenious places are saws, chisels, wooden planes, a set square, spirit levels, hammers, mallets, screwdrivers, wood drills, rulers, etc.
THOMAS was born in 1880. He is a smallish, broad-shouldered man with bright, alert, mischievous eyes. He looks considerably younger than his fifty-six years. His shirt sleeves are rolled up and he is wearing his oldest clothes.
RICHARD is standing some distance away. He has just entered.

THOMAS *hasn't seen him. He works. Slowly he becomes aware of* RICHARD's *presence. He has turned. He stops work.*

THOMAS: Yer wantin' somethin'?

RICHARD: No, no, you carry on like.

THOMAS *works. He feels self-conscious.*

(*Walking towards him:*) A could watch people work all day. Us, yer know. That yer job?

RICHARD *stops near* THOMAS.

THOMAS: Sometimes. Where yer from, laddie?

RICHARD: Newcastle.

THOMAS (*stopping work*): I thought so.

RICHARD: I was wonderin' if yer could tell us where a was like?

THOMAS (*smiling*): The moors, near Guisborough. Yer lost?

RICHARD: Not lost.

THOMAS: What're you askin' for then?

RICHARD: Confirmation, yer know. I'm tryin' to get to Whitby. It's bloody killin' us this.

THOMAS: Have you walked from Newcastle?

RICHARD: Aye, worst luck. I've had a few lifts. Includin' five miles in a Riley.

THOMAS: You've about another fifteen.

RICHARD: Will 'a mekk it by tonight, d'yer reckon?

THOMAS: If it's killin' yer, 'a doubt it.

RICHARD: I shouldn't have opened me gob.

THOMAS: How long've you been out of work?

RICHARD: Two and a half years.

THOMAS: A long time.

RICHARD: Aye, it is, a don't need tellin'. It's bad up in Newcastle. Still bad.

THOMAS: What're you going to Whitby for?

RICHARD: Lookin' for me brother.

THOMAS: Is he there?

ACT ONE 9

RICHARD: Aye, he is, I hope. Me twin like. He left at the back end of August.

THOMAS: Hoping for what?

RICHARD: The trawlers. Fishin', yer know. Or so we'd heard. I believe they go all the way up to Iceland?

THOMAS: He's not come back?

RICHARD: No like. All he's had to do is to write a letter. Which is why he might be in Iceland.

THOMAS *smiles*.

Is there work d'yer know?

THOMAS: I don't.

RICHARD: I asked a bloke in Guisborough – he didn't know either. It's full of ignorance this part of the world. (*Realising.*) Sorry like, a didn't mean you.

THOMAS: I always think of the Geordies as being ignorant. I think you might be wasting your time.

RICHARD: How's that?

THOMAS: If there was work, we'd have heard about it.

RICHARD: You're nearer like?

THOMAS: Yes.

RICHARD: As I've got nearer, that's what I've thought.

THOMAS: It's worth you going to find out.

RICHARD: Aye, thanks mate, thanks.

RICHARD *walks on*.

Thanks, mate. See yer.

THOMAS: What work did you do in Newcastle?

RICHARD *stops and turns*.

RICHARD: The docks, yer know. That's why we thought boats, trawlers. Bit of a dream me'be?

THOMAS *smiles*.

Yer have to have yer dreams, don't yer? I worked a chain horse.

THOMAS *looks blank*.

I was right, you are bloody ignorant.

THOMAS: No, I don't know what a chain horse is.

RICHARD: You've no docks, have yer? With a steep hill up from 'em.

THOMAS: No.

RICHARD: Yer put an extra horse on the front to help pull the load. It takes two horses. At the top yer tekk the chain horse off. Yer go up and down, yo-yo like. Used to. The petrol wagon saw the end of me. (*Angry:*) Me brother wrecked a petrol wagon. I couldn't be bothered.

A slight pause.

(*Calm:*) I saw the point of it all like.

THOMAS: I know.

RICHARD (*challengingly*): D'yer?

A slight pause.

(*Calm:*) Blame me feet, mate, this isn't me talking.

THOMAS (*going to his jacket*): Would you like some chocolate?

RICHARD: No thanks like. Aye, all right, go on.

THOMAS (*taking his jacket*): Are you married?

RICHARD: Aye. Two little lasses. Thankfully only the two, yer know.

THOMAS (*taking a bar of chocolate from his jacket pocket*): Is this the furthest you've looked?

RICHARD: Where d'yer want us to go? Southampton?

THOMAS: It's hard fo'yer.

RICHARD: I sometimes reckon it doesn't do yer any good to talk about what yer already know.

LUCY ELLISON *enters on her bicycle. She is ringing the bell.*
    LUCY *was born in 1919. She is a fresh faced young girl with a wide-eyed expression. There is something of the tomboy about her. She is wearing her school uniform of a blue check, cotton gingham dress over which is an open black coat. She has wellingtons on her feet.*

THOMAS: What do you want, Pet?

LUCY (*coming to a halt*): Come to find you. (*To* RICHARD:) Hello.

RICHARD (*shyly*): Hello.

THOMAS: Has school finished?

LUCY: Hours ago. (*Getting off her bicycle.*) Is that chocolate?

THOMAS: I was just going to share it with –

RICHARD: Richard.

THOMAS: Richard.

LUCY (*taking her bicycle to the wall*): I didn't want any anyway. I hate it. I'll watch you.

LUCY *leans her bicycle against the wall*

(*Turning:*) By the way, Dad. I've felt another premonition. Something's happened to our Rebecca.

THOMAS: Stop it, Lucy.

LUCY (*going to him*): This time I'm absolutely serious. (*To* RICHARD:) Rebecca's my niece. I hate her. (*To* THOMAS:) Don't I?

THOMAS: No.

LUCY (*linking her arm through his*): I'm sure she's come top in a spelling test or something. Or sums. (*To* RICHARD:) Does that ever happen to you?

RICHARD: What d'you mean like?

LUCY: It happens to me.

THOMAS *raises his eyebrows.*

RICHARD: It sounds like yer've a vivid imagination.

THOMAS: Let me give Richard his chocolate.

LUCY *frees her father's arm.* THOMAS *breaks the chocolate into three. He gives a third to* RICHARD.

RICHARD (*taking it*): Am I disturbin' yer?

THOMAS: No.

LUCY: Am I?

THOMAS: Yes.

LUCY: Good.

THOMAS *gives* LUCY *her third of the chocolate.*
The three of them eat in silence for a moment.
RICHARD *raises his hand.*

RICHARD: Thanks. See yer.

THOMAS: See yer.

RICHARD *exits along the road towards Whitby.*

That was rude.

LUCY: What?

THOMAS (*annoyed*): That.

LUCY (*linking her arm through his*): I'm sorry. Forgive me?

THOMAS: No, I don't. I was talking to him.

LUCY *removes her arm.*

LUCY: I didn't stop you talking.

THOMAS (*angry*): That was rude.

A slight pause.

LUCY: Why was it rude, it wasn't –

THOMAS (*interrupting her*): Because I was talking to him.

LUCY: You keep saying that. I didn't stop you.

THOMAS: You'll get a belt in a minute.

LUCY: Don't be silly, Dad. (*Walking away a pace.*) I wish I understood what the fuss was about.

THOMAS: The fuss is because you've been getting very rude lately.

LUCY (*looking him in the eye*): When have I been rude?

THOMAS (*looking her in the eye*): Just now. I mean it, Lucy.

LUCY: I sometimes wish I was a boy. I mean that.

A slight pause.

I'd love to be rude, but you're always telling me off when I haven't been. It's not very fair.

THOMAS: I wish I had treated you like a boy. This would never have happened. (*After a moment's pause:*) I loved you a year ago.

LUCY: Now you're being even sillier.

LUCY *links her arm through his.*

Was Victor this much trouble? I bet Victor was good as gold.

LUCY *kisses* THOMAS *on the cheek.* THOMAS's *eyes flash in both directions.*

(*Insistent:*) Stop looking to see if there's anybody there.

ACT ONE   11

THOMAS (*protesting*): I wasn't.

LUCY: Were.

    LUCY *kisses her father on the cheek.*

    You're so old-fashioned, Daddy.

    LUCY *clings onto his arm.*

    It's not as if we were snoggin'.

THOMAS: Lucy.

LUCY: What?

    A slight pause.

    I remember Victor and Dorothy snoggin'. When I was very little. I didn't know what it was.

    A slight pause.

    I used to snog with my dolly.

THOMAS (*having to hide a smile*): Lucy.

LUCY: I did. Honestly. Don't you believe me?

THOMAS (*putting his hand on hers*): I do. That's the awful thing.

LUCY: I got a splinter in my lips. No, I didn't. That was a joke.

    THOMAS *pats* LUCY's *arm.*

THOMAS: I'm worried about Dorothy and Victor.

LUCY: Why?

THOMAS: Victor's not happy, pet.

LUCY: What's he said?

THOMAS: He hasn't. Not in words.

LUCY: Tell me.

THOMAS (*smiling*): This is where we need a premonition.

LUCY: I agree with you. I think you're right.

    THOMAS *looks at her.*

    I know you think I'm still a girl. I'm not.

THOMAS: Let me ask your advice then.

LUCY (*heartfelt*): Oh please, Dad.

THOMAS (*after a moment's pause*): Maybe we're both imagining it?

LUCY: Rebecca said something interesting.

THOMAS: What?

LUCY: She said her daddy had another country in his eyes. I don't think she knew what she was saying.

THOMAS: When?

LUCY: Oh, a few weeks ago. When he was reading all his Left Book Club stuff. One evening at home. Rebecca was on his knee. Dorothy was upstairs. I was at the table doing my homework. Victor looked far, far away.

THOMAS: He spends too much time with his books. Let's plot together.

LUCY (*excited*): Please.

    A slight pause.

    What's the plot? This is like being Guy Fawkes.

THOMAS *smiles.*

I always knew you were sneaky really. (*Whispering in his ear:*) Sneaky, sneaky, sneaky. (*Her hand suddenly shoots into the sky.*) Look. Look at that.

THOMAS: Where?

LUCY: An aeroplane. See it?

THOMAS *looks.*

THOMAS: Yes.

    The aeroplane passes over their heads. It makes a roar as it goes.
    LUCY *and* THOMAS *instinctively duck down slightly.*
    The aeroplane goes.
    LUCY *and* THOMAS *straighten up.*

LUCY: Bloody hell.

Sudden blackout.

Scene Three

The lights are snapped up.
    Whitby, by the harbour. A flag-stoned quayside.
    Six hours later. Ten o'clock.
    A bright moon is shining.
    The very, very faint sound of the sea. It is like listening to it through a cowrie shell.
    An old wooden fish crate is lying discarded on its own.
    RICHARD *is standing back from the edge of the quay.*
    A slight pause.
    He walks forward, past the fish crate, to

the edge and looks down at the water. He takes the rucksack from his back and puts it down.
   A slight pause.
   A seagull cries. It flies across the quay above his head.
   RICHARD *walks to the fish crate. He picks it up and brings it back. He turns it long side up so that he can use it as a seat. He sits on it, balancing precariously.*
   A seagull cries. It flies back across his head the other way.
   RICHARD *is looking at the harbour.*
   A pause.
   Sudden blackout.

Scene Four
The market town of Guisborough has a long range of hills along its southern edge. The highest point of this, directly above the town, is known as High Cliff.
   The lights are snapped up.
   Guisborough, High Cliff. A few twinkling lights from the town can be seen down below.
   A few seconds later. Ten o'clock.
   A moon is shining.
   VICTOR *is lying sprawled on the grass. He is wearing an overcoat over his suit. There is a hand-written music score in front of him and he has a pencil in his hand. He has a torch.*
   WILFRED FOX *is standing quite a distance away. He has just entered from the surrounding woods.*
   WILFRED *was born in 1910. He is a little, slightly tubby man, with a strong physique. His hair is always dishevelled. He is thickly dressed in all his old clothes, on the top of which is a loosely hanging poacher's coat.*

VICTOR: It's you, Wilf. I couldn't see who it was.

WILFRED: Only me.

WILFRED *walks forward.*

VICTOR: I thought you were a ghost for a minute.

WILFRED: I wondered who it bloody was sittin' up here. (*Squatting down:*) What yer doin'?

VICTOR: Studying this.

WILFRED *pulls the music score towards him.*

As nosey as ever.

WILFRED (*looking at it*): Yer don't know owt if yer not nosey.

WILFRED *scratches his head.*

VICTOR: Satisfied?

WILFRED: What is it?

VICTOR: A music score.

WILFRED: A can see that much.

VICTOR: It's a carol. Christmas carol.

WILFRED: It's a bit of a waste of time is this, Victor.

VICTOR: I'm doing some work with the boys at school.

WILFRED: Yer read this like? Yer hear the music in yer head?

VICTOR: Yes, I do.

WILFRED: No, no. It tekks all sorts t'mekk the world spin. (*Touching a note:*) What's that one?

VICTOR *sings the note.*

Bloody hell, I thought that was opera.

WILFRED *touches another note.* VICTOR *sings it.* WILFRED *touches the note next to it.* VICTOR *sings. This snowballs.* VICTOR *is soon singing the tune of the carol.*

After a short while WILFRED *joins in. He sings a harmony to it in perfect pitch. They sing together for a moment.*

VICTOR: How do you know that?

WILFRED: Everyone knows it. It's 'While Shepherds Watch Their Flocks by Night'.

WILFRED *taps the side of his head.*

VICTOR (*still surprised*): No, how did yer know? I thought I'd found it.

WILFRED: Come t'me when yer want t'know owt.

VICTOR: Tell me.

WILFRED: My old dad used to 'ave a load of these things, when he played the piano. Stuck in the stool like.

VICTOR: What happened to them?

WILFRED: I've got 'em.

VICTOR: You wazzack.

WILFRED: I didn't know yer were interested.

ACT ONE

VICTOR: Can I have them?
WILFRED: Yeh, if yer want 'em.
VICTOR: I'll pay you.
WILFRED: Don't be daft. They're useless.
VICTOR: T'you.
WILFRED: Yer can 'ave 'em, on a promise.
VICTOR: What?
WILFRED: That yer remember my old dad when yer mess about with 'em. My old dad was dear to me.
VICTOR: I want them for school.
WILFRED: Yer too bloody fancy, Victor.
VICTOR: Stop playin' the bloody idiot.
WILFRED (*putting his hand up*): Please, sir, yer shouldn't swear in the classroom.

VICTOR *laughs*.

How's that headmaster of yours?

VICTOR: Don't.
WILFRED: I tripped him up the other day.
VICTOR: Yer what?
WILFRED: Accidentally on purpose.

VICTOR *smiles*.

Flat on his nose. Outside Dixon's pawnshop. Me bloody gun's went again. I'm sick of pawning the bloody thing.

VICTOR (*smiling*): Idiot.
WILFRED: Aye, 'a like bein' an idiot, Victor. It's easier. (*Touching the score:*) No, it's a bit of all right is that.
VICTOR: Have yer bin at the top?
WILFRED: Aye. I'm left wi' me hands now like.

WILFRED *takes a dead rabbit from one of the deep inside pockets of his poacher's coat*.

Four t'night.

VICTOR: Where d'yer take them?
WILFRED: The Seven Stars. The Anchor. I vary it.
VICTOR: What's happened t'yer ferrets?
WILFRED: Had t'sell 'em. Weeks ago.

DOROTHY ELLISON *enters from the town. She is carrying a blanket under her arm.*
DOROTHY *was born in 1902. She is a thin, rather beautiful woman and, although there is something soft about her, she is not frail. She is well-dressed and is wearing a topcoat.*
VICTOR *turns.*

VICTOR: Hello, love.
DOROTHY: Hello. Hello Wilf.
WILFRED (*nodding*): Now then.
DOROTHY: I've brought us all a rug to sit on.

VICTOR *and* WILFRED *stand up.*
DOROTHY *spreads the blanket.*

WILFRED: Yer reckon we're gettin' dirty then, Mrs Ellison?

VICTOR *and* DOROTHY *sit on the blanket.* WILFRED *sits on the grass.*

DOROTHY: Sit on, Wilf.
WILFRED: No, yer all right.
DOROTHY: What were you talking about?
WILFRED: Ferrets.
DOROTHY: Ferrets?
DOROTHY: I was sayin' what buggers the' could be.
DOROTHY: Your language, Wilf.
WILFRED: When the' nip yer fingers.
DOROTHY: My Uncle Victor had ferrets. Not this Victor, another one. In Cambridgeshire. He was the family rogue.
WILFRED: Oh aye?
DOROTHY: Yes, I rather liked him. (*To* VICTOR:) Don't you remember?
VICTOR: Mmm.
DOROTHY (*to* WILFRED): He was a gamekeeper. The rest of my family were books.

WILFRED *nods.*
A slight pause.

Isn't it rather cold sitting here?

VICTOR: I was coming back.

A slight pause.

DOROTHY: Has Victor told you Rebecca had an operation this afternoon?

WILFRED: No, the bugger didn't.

DOROTHY: It seems to have gone very well, we gather. We have been very worried.

WILFRED: What's the lass done?

VICTOR: Cut her finger.

WILFRED (*pulling a face*): Badly like?

VICTOR: Unfortunately.

DOROTHY: The surgeon's very highly regarded, so we're optimistic. (*To* VICTOR:) Isn't he?

VICTOR: Yes.

DOROTHY: Mr Smith, you know. Medicine has been in the family for generations, apparently. I've talked to his daughter in the butchers.

WILFRED: She'll be all right?

VICTOR: Yes.

DOROTHY: Mr Smith wouldn't let us see her this evening. That's understandable. (*Turning to him*:) I'm surprised you didn't say anything, Victor.

VICTOR: It's early days yet. We don't want to build our hopes up.

DOROTHY: We thought it was remarkable how far surgery had advanced.

VICTOR: She has to have her arm in a splint for a month.

DOROTHY: It's a new operation.

WILFRED: It's goin' t'cost yer a penny or two.

VICTOR: Mr Smith's doing it for nothing.

DOROTHY (*jumping in*): We've money put by for a rainy day. It's what everybody should save for.

WILFRED: Them that can like.

DOROTHY: Everybody can save at least something.

WILFRED: Yer might find us arguin' wi' that like.

DOROTHY: I can argue, too.

WILFRED: A won't, 'cos o' your lass.

DOROTHY: Victor and I have always been very careful with money.

WILFRED *closes his mouth. He holds his lips together with his fingers.*

VICTOR: Give over, Wilf.

DOROTHY: Wilf knows I'm not accusing him.

WILFRED (*still holding his lips*): Yer've money t'be careful with, Mrs Ellison.

VICTOR: Stop it, Wilf.

WILFRED (*taking his fingers away*): You're as bad an' all.

VICTOR: He's doing it for nothing because it's an operation he's not done before.

DOROTHY (*trying not to be upset*): He hasn't done it for nothing, Victor.

VICTOR: He can't guarantee success.

DOROTHY *looks down.*
A slight pause.

WILFRED: If yer pull the other one yer'll find it rings.

VICTOR (*firmly*): What?

WILFRED: Yer really believe that, don't yer.

VICTOR: I believe what I'm told by people who know better.

WILFRED (*challengingly*): Tut.

VICTOR: You're off you're head, Wilf.

WILFRED: I am, am I.

DOROTHY (*looking up*): Let's not argue.

WILFRED: What if it hadn't been your lass, but somebody else's? Not a school teacher's?

DOROTHY: I think you've got the wrong idea.

WILFRED: I have, have I?

DOROTHY: Victor's done more than anyone in this town for people like you.

WILFRED: People like me?

DOROTHY (*apologetically*): I can't help the words I choose sometimes.

WILFRED: Aye, a know.

A slight pause.

VICTOR: Why d'you think I became a teacher, Wilf?

WILFRED (*shrugging*): Search me.

VICTOR: I've pushed for scholarships.

ACT ONE 15

WILFRED: Tut.

DOROTHY: And what's more we've bought shoes for children.

VICTOR (*really angry*): Stop it.

DOROTHY: I won't. It's time he knew these things. We've bought shoes and books and pencils for children. For one family in particular. A very bright boy. His family have ever so little, but they've tried. It is quite terrible the way you speak to us, Wilf.

WILFRED *holds his lips together with his fingers.*

It doesn't do to make a joke of it all the time. It doesn't befit you. (*To* VICTOR:) Does it?

VICTOR: Wilf's only not saying what he thinks.

DOROTHY: He seems to be saying it very precisely.

VICTOR (*he has seen someone in the surrounding trees*): Away.

WILFRED *looks. He pushes the rabbit back into his coat. He stands up and walks away.*
    POLICE CONSTABLE PRICE *enters. He is wearing his uniform.*
    PRICE *was born in 1886. He is a large, squarely-built man with a moustache.*
    PRICE *has a flashlight. He turns it off.*

PRICE: Good evening.

VICTOR: Good evening, constable.

WILFRED (*trying not to be nervous*): Now then, Willy.

PRICE *nods.*

PRICE: I'm glad to see you as a matter of fact, Wilfred. Given that Mr and Mrs Ellison don't go poaching.

WILFRED: Yer never know, d'yer?

PRICE: I think I've a shrewd idea in this case. (*To* VICTOR *and* DOROTHY:) I'm sorry about this. (*To* WILFRED:) Is it just rabbits?

WILFRED: We tried takin' the plough-horse, but he didn't want t'go.

PRICE: The Squire up there's been 'avin' a lot of trouble, Mr and Mrs Ellison. (*To* WILFRED:) Where's t'nights thievery? I don't want t'see 'em if they're rabbits. They're wild. It's the geese I'm after. Someone's been gettin' a bit above themselves.

WILFRED: It's just rabbits, yer know that.

PRICE: There's more rabbits in The Seven Stars some nights than customers. There can't be many left.

A slight pause.

These Christmas geese then. What we gonna do about it?

DOROTHY: How many have gone?

PRICE: Half a dozen so far.

DOROTHY: Is it you, Wilf?

WILFRED: Look, it ain't me.

PRICE: I think a might believe yer, Wilf, if yer weren't such a bloody liar. Who, then?

WILFRED: Yer must think a'm stupid, even if a knew.

PRICE: I don't think you're stupid, Wilfred, I know you are.

WILFRED *goes red.*

I'd like one left f' the wife t'buy on December the twenty-third. So, yer can tell Colin Gibson and his scrawny mate, that I know. Got it?

WILFRED (*quietly*): Yes.

PRICE: Has it sunk in? I know it has to fight its way through layers of ignorance.

WILFRED (*he can't restrain himself*): Fuck off.

VICTOR (*quickly standing up*): I'll see it's done, constable.

PRICE (*his finger pointing*): I'll do you one day, my lad.

A pause.

VICTOR: I'll see it's done.

PRICE: Thank you, Mr Ellison. If I see them, I'll have to charge them.

A slight pause.

(*To* WILFRED:) Do you wonder why I've been promoted?

PRICE *turns the flashlight on.*

Yer reckon I'll go t'heaven, d'yer, Wilf?

WILFRED: Aye, Willy.

PRICE: Goodnight.
VICTOR: Goodnight, constable.
DOROTHY: Goodnight.

PRICE *exits the way he came, back towards the town.*
After a moment VICTOR *sits again.*

Was it you?

WILFRED: I went up with 'em one night. We couldn't catch the bloody things, there were feathers everywhere. They've been goin' back with a net.

DOROTHY: Why, Wilf?

WILFRED (*walking towards* VICTOR): Why is glass opaque?

DOROTHY (*mystified*): So that you can see through it.

WILFRED (*looking at her*): Glass isn't opaque, Mrs Ellison.

DOROTHY: I'm sorry, you're confusing me.

A slight pause.

I wish you'd call me Dorothy.

A slight pause.

It's stealing.

WILFRED (*squatting down*): Aye, mekks it excitin'.

A slight pause.

DOROTHY (*she wants to understand*): It's against the law, taking what doesn't belong to you.

A slight pause.

What do you think, Victor?

VICTOR: He knows anything I would think.

VICTOR *winks at* WILFRED.
WILFRED *smiles.*

DOROTHY: What was that?

VICTOR: Nothing, love.

DOROTHY: You did something. You did something behind my back.

VICTOR: I didn't. Don't be silly. Don't get so upset.

DOROTHY: You did. (*To* WILFRED:) What did he do?

WILFRED: Nothing, Dorothy.

DOROTHY: He did. I wish to know.

VICTOR: I winked at him.

DOROTHY: Why? (*After a moment's pause.*) Why, Victor?

VICTOR: Because I wanted to, love.

DOROTHY: I don't know why, I must say. It just isn't good enough to say you wanted to. I want to do all sorts of things.

VICTOR: Let it rest.

DOROTHY: I won't let it rest. I'm always the one who does that. It just isn't fair. Not fair at all.

VICTOR (*annoyed*): Oh, stop it for God's sake.

DOROTHY: No, I won't stop it.

VICTOR: We're in front of Wilf.

DOROTHY: Wilf might as well hear.

A slight pause.

VICTOR: I winked at him, that was all.

DOROTHY: I know I'm naïve, it just isn't fair. But there has to be right and wrong sometimes. Someone has to stand up for that.

VICTOR: Nobody's saying the opposite?

DOROTHY: Then why wink, Victor?

VICTOR: We're embarrassing Wilf.

WILFRED: I am a bit like.

Silence.

DOROTHY: And it's no good thinking it doesn't matter.

Silence.
    WILFRED *stands up.*

VICTOR: See yer, Wilf.

WILFRED: Aye, see yer.

WILFRED *exits towards the town.*
Silence.

VICTOR: Aren't you cold?

DOROTHY (*still furious*): I'm hot. I'm bloody hot. And why are you always up here?

Silence.

Meeting your friends without me.

Silence.

Why don't we make love anymore? I miss you next to me. Your father's noticed.

A slight pause.

Lucy with her bloody impossible questions all evening.

VICTOR: I like it up here.

DOROTHY (*trying not to be upset*): I don't know about us anymore, Victor.

VICTOR *takes off his overcoat. He puts it round* DOROTHY*'s shoulders.*

You'll be cold now.

DOROTHY: It doesn't matter.

A slight pause.

That seems to express it very well.

A slight pause.

Why don't we play the piano together? Like we used to in Cambridge? I used to enjoy those evenings so. I felt like Queen Victoria.

A slight pause.

Have those evenings gone forever?

A slight pause.

Why won't you let me look at your music?

VICTOR: It's no good.

A slight pause.

DOROTHY: That seems so negative.

VICTOR: When it's good, I'll tell you.

A pause.

DOROTHY: I feel like an outsider. Is that how musicians write – by being peculiar?

A slight pause.

By having feelings and disappointments they can't explain.

VICTOR: I think any artist wants to get his own back on the world.

DOROTHY: On me?

A slight pause.

VICTOR: Not you, love.

A slight pause.

DOROTHY: I've always thought of music as a joyous thing.

VICTOR: It's irrelevant.

A slight pause.

DOROTHY: It's not irrelevant. Not to us.

VICTOR: There's too many people having too hard a life. (*Instantly changing his mind*:) That was silly.

DOROTHY *puts her hand inside his coat. She runs her fingers beneath the top of his trousers.*

DOROTHY: If we could start making love again. Maybe we'd feel better?

A slight pause.

I miss your penis. If we got one of those rude books out again?

DOROTHY *takes her hand away.*

What you don't seem to realise, is that I want an escape too. (*Trying not to be upset*:) It's easy for you, you don't care about appearances. I know that's very modern. (*Tears coming into her eyes*:) I have to walk down the street knowing that people are looking at me.

VICTOR *looks at her.*

And they are, Victor. Please let's go to London.

VICTOR: Nobody's looking at you.

DOROTHY (*insistent*): Yes, they are. There are eyes in every corner. In London I would be modern. Everyone's modern there.

DOROTHY *wipes some tears from her eyes.*

I'd let you have affairs in London, as long as I could keep you.

VICTOR *looks down.*

I expect you do. Though I've no sort of proof. Which I could easily have done. I am right, aren't I?

VICTOR *looks up.*

I feel the eyes on me in this town, knowing that. Don't worry, I haven't told anybody else.

A slight pause.

I should also say that I don't want to know who she is.

A pause.
    Sudden blackout.

Scene Five

The lights are snapped up.
The moors. The Whitby road. The drystone wall is now complete.
Five days later, Saturday, October 10th. Midday.
The sky is full of cloud. It is raining.
WILFRED's old bicycle is resting against the wall. Beside it, on the grass verge, there is a large hessian sack with something in it.
WILFRED is sitting on the wall. He is wet.
RICHARD is standing a short distance away. He has his knapsack on his back. He is wet. He has just entered.

WILFRED: It's bloody weather for October, isn't it?

RICHARD: Aye like.

WILFRED (*taking an egg from the pocket of his poacher's coat*): Want an egg?

He throws it to RICHARD. RICHARD catches it.

RICHARD: Where d'yer get these?

WILFRED: Pilfered 'em.

WILFRED takes another egg from his pocket. He cracks it on the wall, tilts his head back, opens his mouth, and swallows the contents.
RICHARD has walked to the wall. He has done the same.

(*Taking a third egg from his pocket:*) Want another?

RICHARD (*pulling a face*): One's enough like.

WILFRED *cracks the egg. He eats the contents.*
RICHARD watches him.

That'd make us feel sick like.

RICHARD clambers onto, and sits on the wall.
WILFRED takes a bottle of stout from one of the inside pockets of his coat. He takes the stopper out with his teeth. He drinks.

WILFRED (*passing the bottle*): Where've yer come from?

RICHARD: Whitby.

RICHARD drinks.

WILFRED: I went t'bloody Whitby.

RICHARD (*holding the bottle*): I was lookin' for me brother. He's never there, of course.

WILFRED *holds his hand out.*
RICHARD *gives him the bottle.*

Me twin brother, yer know.

WILFRED: No, I didn't know yer'd got a brother. What's yer name?

RICHARD: Richard.

WILFRED: Wilf. Now then.

RICHARD (*smiling shyly*): Now then.

WILFRED (*jumping down from the wall*): What happened to 'im?

RICHARD: From Newcastle t'Whitby, from Whitby to Spain.

WILFRED *lies full length on the grass verge.*

Are you all right, mate?

WILFRED: T' Spain?

RICHARD: Aye. I reckoned he might be in Iceland.

WILFRED: Looks like 'e's gone the wrong way.

RICHARD: Aye, that's what I thought. There's a war on, yer know.

WILFRED *sits up, he drinks from the bottle. He changes position, leaning back against the wall.*

WILFRED (*passing him the bottle*): Yer married?

RICHARD (*taking it*): Aye. You?

WILFRED: Yeh.

RICHARD: Any bairns?

WILFRED: Yeh.

RICHARD: How many?

WILFRED: Two. Two boys.

RICHARD: I've got two lasses.

WILFRED: My biggest lad's just started school.

RICHARD: Mine are littler than that.

WILFRED: Yer gonna finish it?

RICHARD: Aye. Ta.

WILFRED: If yer not, I'll 'ave it.

RICHARD *drinks, finishes the bottle of stout.*
　WILFRED *stands up. He takes the hessian sack and walks away a few feet. He turns the sack upside down. A swan tumbles out. It is dead, but unmarked, and perfectly white.*
　RICHARD *looks in disbelief.*
(*Holding up the long neck*:) Isn't she beautiful?

RICHARD: Where did you get that?

WILFRED: Along there, there's a reservoir.

RICHARD: What yer goin' to do with it?

WILFRED: Eat it. A couldn't stop meself. Know what 'a mean?

RICHARD: Yeh, but a swan, yer know.

WILFRED: I've got t'pluck the bloody thing yet. Tekk hours.

WILFRED *lays the neck on the ground.*

I hated doin' it.

RICHARD: Yer shouldn't have done it.

WILFRED (*looking at him*): Yer think yer better than me, d'yer?

RICHARD: I didn't say that, mate.

WILFRED: What did yer say?

RICHARD: Nothin'.

WILFRED *stands up.*

WILFRED: I'll break that fuckin' bottle over your fuckin' head.

RICHARD *goes red.*

RICHARD (*nervously*): I don't fight.

WILFRED (*pointing at himself*): I do, I do. I get sick of bein' taken f'a fuckin' idiot.

A slight pause.

RICHARD: I never said you were an idiot.

A slight pause.
　WILFRED *kneels down. He starts to stroke the swan.*

You're strange.

WILFRED (*bellowing*): Yer what?

RICHARD (*raising his hands*): I didn't say anythin'.

WILFRED (*jumping up, going to him*): Get off that wall.

RICHARD (*he is not sure what to say*): No.

WILFRED: Get off, or I'll push you off.

A moment's pause.
　RICHARD *gets off the wall. He stands.*

What did yer say?

RICHARD: Listen, mate, I've said, I don't want a fight with yer.

A slight pause.

It's best if I go like before we have trouble.

A slight pause.

All right?

WILFRED *starts to cry. He turns his head away. He sobs.*
　A long, long pause.
　WILFRED *turns, he lifts his head up.*

Yer should walk somewhere, mate.

A slight pause.

Yer never know what yer puttin' up with, do yer? (*After a moment's pause*:) Till yer've put up with it. Or yer've walked somewhere.

A slight pause.

Yer scared us, I can tell yer. I'll remember today.

A slight pause.

All right?

WILFRED: Yeh.

A slight pause.

It's me, I'm goin' mad.

A slight pause.

I'm fuckin' violent. 'A weren't like, when 'a were a bairn, just after the war.

RICHARD: Yer lose yer dad?

WILFRED: No.

RICHARD: I lost mine like.

WILFRED: It didn't 'elp 'im; 'e died a few years after.

RICHARD: Maybe I'll walk to France to find his grave. (*After a moment's pause*:) I hardly remember him, yer know.

A slight pause.

It's important. History. Our lives.

WILFRED (*heartfelt*): Yeh, but the' think a'm stupid.

RICHARD: I weren't meaning school, mate. Yer have to look at history for yourself.

WILFRED: Yeh, but if I'm stupid.

RICHARD: They want yer to think you're stupid.

A slight pause.

WILFRED: It don't make no bloody sense.

A slight pause.

Yer from Newcastle?

RICHARD: Aye.

WILFRED: Yer goin' back?

RICHARD: Aye, a suppose so.

WILFRED: What fo'?

RICHARD: For me bairns, mate, and me wife. (*After a moment's pause*:) I went to Whitby for me dreams. To tell you the truth like, it's been a nightmare.

A slight pause.

See yer.

WILFRED: See yer, mate.

RICHARD *walks away.*

Take me bicycle, if yer want.

RICHARD: No thanks like. Aye, all right, go on.

RICHARD *gets on the bicycle, he has his foot on the pedal.*

Yer sure yer sure?

WILFRED: Yeh, why not. Watch the front brake, it doesn't work.

RICHARD *bicycles off towards Guisborough.*
WILFRED *watches him go.*
A slight pause.
Sudden blackout.

Scene Six

The lights are snapped up.
The garden of the Chaloner Hospital.
Sunday, November 1st.
The sun is shining.
REBECCA ELLISON *is sitting in a wheelchair under the boughs of a tree. She is wearing a white nightdress and a dressing-gown, and there is a blanket over her knees and legs. Her left arm is in a sling, it keeps her hand on her right shoulder. She is reading a book.*
REBECCA *was born in 1928. She is a pretty little girl with fair hair.*
PEGGY, *in a white coat, is kneeling on the grass in front of her.* PEGGY *is holding a pair of spectacles.*

PEGGY: What are you reading?

REBECCA: *Oliver Twist* by Charles Dickens.

PEGGY: What's it about?

REBECCA: Oliver, who has terrible things happen to him. You must have read it?

PEGGY: Yes, I have.

REBECCA: Mummy says I have to be clever.

PEGGY (*putting the spectacles on*): May I look at your hand, Rebecca?

REBECCA: Yes.

PEGGY *helps* REBECCA *take her arm from the sling.*
REBECCA*'s forearm is in a long splint which pushes her wrist into thirty degrees of flexion. The whole forearm, and especially the hand, are heavily bandaged.*

Why don't we put Oliver on the grass?

PEGGY *takes the book from* REBECCA*'s lap.*

It still smells a bit. (*Smelling it:*) Pooh.

PEGGY *examines the hand, delving very carefully with a pair of tweezers into the bandages across her palm to reveal the bottoms of her fingers.*

PEGGY: This hand needs a very good wash. (REBECCA *looks as if she is about to move them.*) Keep your fingers still, love.

REBECCA: Yes.

PEGGY (*after a moment's pause*): It's healed very nicely where the stitches were.

REBECCA: Am I still a guinea-pig?

A slight pause.

PEGGY: Is your wrist aching?

ACT ONE 21

REBECCA: A little bit. I've got used to it.

PEGGY: The splint can come off tomorrow.

REBECCA (*excited*): Can it? Oh, good. Just in time for bonfire night.

PEGGY (*still concentrating on her work*): You'll need to be here for another six weeks yet, Beccy.

REBECCA: Don't they have fireworks in a hospital?

PEGGY: I think I might be able to find some. One or two because you're special.

DOROTHY *enters. She is wearing an autumn coat.*

REBECCA: Mummy.

DOROTHY: Hello.

PEGGY (*leaving* REBECCA's *hand, sitting back on her haunches. Brightly*): Hello, Mrs Ellison.

In the same movement PEGGY *stands up. She takes her spectacles off and puts them in her coat pocket.*

REBECCA: I'm going to have a bonfire.

PEGGY: Fireworks, Beccy. If we had a bonfire we might set the hospital alight.

DOROTHY (*smiling*): That's nice, isn't it?

REBECCA: Yes.

DOROTHY: Thank you.

PEGGY: There are three or four children in the public wards who could come too. It's strictly against the rules.

DOROTHY: Mr Ellison's not called here, by any chance?

PEGGY: I was expecting him with you.

REBECCA: Where's Daddy?

DOROTHY: In a minute. (*After a moment's pause:*) I'd like a word with you, if I may.

PEGGY *and* DOROTHY *walk away.*

REBECCA: Where are you going?

DOROTHY: Mummy won't be a moment, darling.

The two women have stopped.

PEGGY: You're upset?

DOROTHY (*calmly*): No. yes.

PEGGY (*gently*): Why don't you tell me what it is?

DOROTHY: I know what I'm going to say must seem a frightful imposition. A cheek, almost.

PEGGY: Yes?

DOROTHY: I have very few women friends. It's so silly, I'm so worried. Victor – Mr Ellison's – gone.

PEGGY *is not sure how to react.*

PEGGY: He's gone. Where's he gone?

DOROTHY: I don't know.

PEGGY: Perhaps he wanted to be by himself for a few days.

DOROTHY (*her voice rising slightly*): Why should he?

A slight pause.

He's not been to see Rebecca?

PEGGY: No.

DOROTHY (*her voice rising*): How could he do this to a child?

PEGGY: I don't know, Mrs Ellison.

REBECCA: Shall I put my arm back in the sling?

PEGGY: Yes. Be careful.

DOROTHY (*after a moment's pause*): I thought if I had a word with you it might make me feel better. It has already. I feel so, so alone without him.

PEGGY: When did he go?

DOROTHY: Yesterday morning. There was nothing. No note. Not anything.

REBECCA *is putting her arm back into the sling.*

PEGGY (*calling to her*): Are you managing?

REBECCA: Yes.

PEGGY: Don't move those fingers, will you.

REBECCA: No.

DOROTHY: Why did you say he might want to be by himself?

PEGGY (*after a moment's pause*): Men like Mr Ellison do from time to time.

DOROTHY: Have I been cruel to him?

PEGGY (*after a moment's pause*): No.

A slight pause.

DOROTHY: You see, doctor, I think he might have gone to Spain. Now I know that sounds ridiculous. Victor's a socialist. I'm not, I'm afraid. These socialist people are sometimes very selfish, and Victor is easily led. He goes to meetings.

A slight pause.

If he has gone to Spain, there is a war being fought. It will do them no good, I think. (*After a moment's pause*:) But cost people money. And possibly their lives.

REBECCA *picks up her book. She starts to read.*

If we became friends I'd tell you the whole truth. It really is just terrible. (*After a moment's pause*:) I've felt, forgive me, that I've been getting to know you.

A slight pause.

PEGGY: I don't know what to say, Mrs Ellison.

DOROTHY: I think I'm beginning to hate men. (*After a moment's pause*:) Yes, I do, I hate men, Dr Smith.

PEGGY: Have you tried telephoning his school?

DOROTHY: It's Sunday.

PEGGY: Yes, of course. (*After a moment's pause*:) I obviously didn't know Victor.

DOROTHY: No. I'm sorry. (*After a moment's pause*:) What shall I tell Beccy?

PEGGY: I wouldn't say anything for the time being.

DOROTHY (*smiling*): I haven't asked about her.

PEGGY (*smiling*): She's doing just fine.

DOROTHY: We'll know tomorrow whether the suture's held?

PEGGY: Yes. My father's big day.

DOROTHY: What next?

PEGGY: The hard work begins, to get a very tired finger active again. It's an extensive programme. Beccy's going to have to work really really hard.

REBECCA (*looking up from her book*): What's that about me?

DOROTHY: Mummy shan't be long.

REBECCA *reads her book.*
PEGGY *holds up a pair of crossed fingers.*

PEGGY: Let us hope, Mrs Ellison.

DOROTHY: If there are problems, what might they be?

A slight pause.

Shouldn't I ask?

PEGGY: We think the main thing to watch for is if the tendon itself has adhered to the tunnel in the finger down which it glides. And the profundus muscle will need re-educating. The idea of the splint is to halt muscle and flexor tendon function.

DOROTHY: Yes.

PEGGY: But in halting the function you immediately set up the chances of adherence. Because the tendon is still. Like any wound it will repair and fasten to its surrounding surface. Which is why we must get it moving. Get it gliding, to stop that. We couldn't do it before the fourth week because the tendon repair would snap under even the tiniest amount of pressure from flexion.

DOROTHY: Yes.

PEGGY: If active, and later passive, movement of Beccy's finger fails to produce improvement –

A telephone starts to ring in one of the adjacent offices.

I'm sorry, there's my telephone ringing, I must go. But it is possible to try tenolysis as a secondary procedure.

PEGGY *dashes off.*
REBECCA *looks up from her book.*

REBECCA: My tendon's been a lot of trouble, Mummy.

DOROTHY: Yes.

DOROTHY *walks to* REBECCA.

REBECCA: Would you read to me?

DOROTHY *sits on the grass.*

(*Passing her the book, her finger on the place*:) From there.

ACT ONE 23

DOROTHY (*reads*): The Dodger sighed again, and resumed his pipe: as did Charley Bates. They both smoked, for some seconds, in silence.
'I suppose you don't even know what a prig is?' said the Dodger mournfully.
'I think I know that,' replied Oliver, looking up. 'It's a th –; you're one, are you not?' inquired Oliver, checking himself.
'I am,' replied the Dodger. 'I'd scorn to be anything else.' Mr Dawkins gave his hat a ferocious cock, after delivering this sentiment, and looked at Master Bates, as if to denote that he would feel obliged by his saying anything to the contrary.
'I am,' repeated the Dodger. 'So's Charley. So's Fagin. So's Sykes. So's Nancy. So's Bet. So we all are, down to the dog. And he's the downiest one of the lot!'

Sudden blackout.

Scene Seven

A spotlight is snapped up.
The attic at the Ellisons' house. A light bulb hangs from the cobwebbed rafters of the low ceiling.
Christmas Eve.
THOMAS *is sitting on the only chair. In front of him is a small wooden box in which there are letters. He has one letter in his hand.*
LUCY *is behind him. She is wearing a pair of trousers and a shirt which are far too big for her. Her hair is pushed up inside a cap. She is leaning on* THOMAS *with her arms around her neck.*

LUCY: I've brought you a hat.

LUCY *stands up. She puts a paper hat on his head.*

THOMAS: Don't I look silly?

LUCY: That's the idea.

He takes it off.

Oh, don't.

THOMAS (*putting it back on*): I must look almost as foolish as you.

LUCY: They're Victor's. Like them?

THOMAS: No.

LUCY: Why not. What do I look like?

THOMAS: A boy. I wish you wouldn't, Lucy.

LUCY: It does you good. Beccy's helping with the Christmas tree.

THOMAS (*smiling*): I will come down.

LUCY *is looking at him.*

A pause.

I will.

A pause.

LUCY: No, you won't.

A pause.

THOMAS: I will.

A pause.

(*Picking up a few letters:*) I was reading Victor's letters.

He puts them down.
A pause.

LUCY: No, you won't, Daddy.

THOMAS: The Cambridge ones. Looking for a clue.

LUCY: What is the point of that?

THOMAS: I loved him.

A slight pause.

Victor has had most of my life, Lucy.

A slight pause.

LUCY: No, you won't, Daddy.

THOMAS: You're behaving as if you don't care.

LUCY: He's gone.

THOMAS *starts to take the paper hat off.*

Leave it on your head, and do as you're told.

THOMAS *puts the hat back.*
A pause.

(*With* THOMAS's *line:*) I don't see the point of sitting up here.

THOMAS (*with* LUCY's *line*): I don't want to talk about it, Lucy.

A pause.

LUCY: I'm not going.

A slight pause.
Stillness.
The lights fade to half-light.
ELIZABETH *and* EDWARD *enter.*

They hum the opening folk tune.
THOMAS *and* LUCY *leave.*

Scene Eight

The lights travel up.
A small wooded coppice adjoining ELIZABETH BRADLEY'*s house by the river Thames in Twickenham.*
Saturday, October 9th, 1920.
A warm autumn sunlight is filtering through the trees.
EDWARD LONGRESSE *is lying asleep on the ground, he has his head on a large yellow cushion.*
EDWARD *was born in 1902. He is a tall, good looking boy with fair hair. He is wearing white trousers and jacket, and a white shirt.*
ELIZABETH BRADLEY, *with a long peacock feather in her hand, is standing some distance away. She has just entered.*
ELIZABETH *was born in 1874. She is a petite woman, but she has none of the fayness that might go with that. Her face has quite a hard edge to it. She cares little for her appearance, but nevertheless her clothes are fine.*
ELIZABETH *walks forward, she tickles his chin with the feather.* EDWARD *opens his eyes.*

ELIZABETH: Here you are, Edward, this is a surprise.

EDWARD (*he is still*): I trust a nice surprise, Aunt.

ELIZABETH: Yes, I shall sit with you.

ELIZABETH *starts to sit.* EDWARD *jumps up.*

EDWARD: Would you like the cushion? I stole it from the drawing-room.

ELIZABETH (*sitting*): You're young, you keep it, dear.

EDWARD *sits.*

Yes, Pickles would tell you I've been lunching with that awful Mrs Wilson.

EDWARD: She said.

ELIZABETH: Of course if you'd told me you were coming I would have cancelled the thing.

EDWARD: I didn't know until this morning.

ELIZABETH (*strongly*): I would have telephoned her. (*Smiling:*) Goodness me, I haven't told you off since you were fourteen. What had you done then, I wonder?

EDWARD: Put itching-powder in Pickles's vests.

ELIZABETH *laughs.*

ELIZABETH: Yes, Mrs Wilson has one of those toy thingummies, Edward. What are they called? You know.

EDWARD (*shaking his head*): I don't. What?

ELIZABETH: It sits on her lap like a spare hand.

EDWARD: A dog.

ELIZABETH *makes a playful swipe at him with her hand.*

ELIZABETH: It's a special dog. A special thingummy.

EDWARD: You're dotty, Aunt.

ELIZABETH: She gloats over it like a meal. It quite put me off my shepherd's pie.

EDWARD *laughs.*

So, Edward, here you are. Haven't you a telephone?

EDWARD: I thought you'd be delighted to see me.

ELIZABETH: I am, dear, I am. That's why I'm annoyed.

ELIZABETH *holds out her hand.* EDWARD *takes it.*

I've missed you.

EDWARD: Me, too.

ELIZABETH (*smiling*): Isn't that a little like a lie?

EDWARD: Don't be silly.

ELIZABETH *laughs. Their hands part.*

ELIZABETH: What do we do if we live alone like Mrs Wilson?

EDWARD: Be doggyless.

ELIZABETH: I think so. The truth is I've given up caring about what the world thinks about me. (*Smiling.*) You've changed, Edward. Haven't you?

EDWARD (*smiling*): What are you talking about?

ACT ONE 25

ELIZABETH: Good. I'm very pleased.

EDWARD: I've only been away for a month.

ELIZABETH: We sometimes change more in one day than we do in ten years.

EDWARD: What nonsense.

ELIZABETH: Is it?

EDWARD: What nonsense.

ELIZABETH (*after a moment's pause*): Yes, dear, I'm sure you're right.

A slight pause.

What about some lemonade?

EDWARD: I'm fine, Elizabeth.

EDWARD *smiles*.

ELIZABETH: That smile is hiding something. I'm not sure what. Forget my little jealousies. Did you have luncheon?

EDWARD: Yes, Aunt, in a public-house. A very rowdy place, fully of jolly men singing.

ELIZABETH: Oh dear.

EDWARD: No, it was wonderful. I did feel foolish, being on my own. And having a car which everyone looked at. And then spending over an hour taking rides. And then not feeling foolish, but very upper-class. And trying to explain that I wasn't. And after the rides yet another drink of beer, and then another. Which is why I was sleeping. This is nineteen-twenty, well and truly.

ELIZABETH (*smiling*): Take care of your youth. Don't have age hurry you.

EDWARD: I will.

EDWARD *smiles*.

ELIZABETH: Such a reticent smile.

EDWARD (*laughing*): What are you talking about?

ELIZABETH: A smile full of doubts. When I was eighteen I wanted to rush.

EDWARD: I can't think of you at eighteen.

ELIZABETH: I was beautiful.

EDWARD: Like Mother?

ELIZABETH: No, much, much more than your Mother.

EDWARD: Mother was lumpy?

ELIZABETH *makes a playful swipe at him with her hand*.

ELIZABETH (*smiling*): As lumpy as a fish.

EDWARD: I shall tell her.

ELIZABETH *laughs. She takes* EDWARD's *head and places it in her lap*.

ELIZABETH: So, Edward, tell me about Cambridge?

EDWARD: What is there to say?

ELIZABETH: Tell me everything.

EDWARD (*brightly*): Apart from the truth that I hate it.

ELIZABETH (*surprised*): Oh?

EDWARD: I don't hate it. It hates me.

ELIZABETH: Isn't Cambridge a collection of buildings like any other.

A slight pause.

Places are what we make of them. Not they us.

A slight pause.

How long have we known each other, Edward? As adults, not as adult and child?

EDWARD: Since I put the itching-powder in Pickles's vests.

ELIZABETH *makes a playful swipe at him with her hand. She moves his head and stands up*.

ELIZABETH: Have you run short of money already?

A slight pause.

(*Walking away a pace:*) I shan't know unless you tell me?

ELIZABETH *turns and looks at him*.

Don't hate yourself, whatever it is. Hatred is such an ugly thing.

EDWARD (*quite enjoying it*): I'm in love. With a boy. It's beastly.

ELIZABETH: Boys are there to be loved.

EDWARD: Are they?

ELIZABETH: Sometimes by girls, sometimes not.

EDWARD: I thought you might be shocked.

ELIZABETH: I cannot pretend it's what I expected to hear.

EDWARD: What would you do?

ELIZABETH: I'd do whatever I wanted, dear.

EDWARD: I haven't spoken to him.

ELIZABETH: Is he at Kings?

EDWARD: Yes, Aunt. He's a working-class boy.

ELIZABETH: Is that his appeal?

EDWARD (*brightly*): I think I might jolly well like being one of those.

ELIZABETH *smiles. She walks to him.*

ELIZABETH: I fell in love with our post-boy.

EDWARD (*shocked*): Aunt Elizabeth.

ELIZABETH (*leaning forward*): As did your mother. But I was the one who saw his bottom.

ELIZABETH *puts a finger to her lips.*

Don't you dare tell anyone that. It was said in confidence.

EDWARD (*calling, not very loudly*): Pick-les.

ELIZABETH: Edward, you promised.

EDWARD: I didn't. (*The same tone:*) Pick-les.

ELIZABETH: Edward.

EDWARD: What?

They are looking at one another.
ELIZABETH *makes a dive for him.*
EDWARD *stands up.*

(*Still quietly:*) Pick-les, Pickles, Pickles, Pick-les.

ELIZABETH (*looking up at him*): Oh, you are naughty. I shall tell you nothing else.

EDWARD: How old were you?

ELIZABETH *is silent.*

Pick-les.

ELIZABETH: Nineteen, Edward.

ELIZABETH *suddenly laughs.*

It was a spotty bottom.

EDWARD: How on earth did you see it?

ELIZABETH (*putting a finger in front of her lips*): Sssh.

ELIZABETH *motions.* EDWARD *bends his head.* ELIZABETH *whispers something in his ear.* EDWARD *straightens up.*

EDWARD (*a sing-song voice*): Pick-les. Elizabeth saw twenty spotty bottoms, swimming in the river.

ELIZABETH (*jumping up*): Stop it, Edward.

EDWARD (*getting louder*): Pickles. Pickles.

ELIZABETH (*jumping up, trying to put her hand in front of his mouth*): Stop it, don't, stop it.

EDWARD: Pickles. Pickles.

ELIZABETH: Stop it.

They stop.
ELIZABETH *laughs.*

Oh dear.

EDWARD (*looking about*): Has someone pruned the apple trees?

ELIZABETH: Yes, I got Jack to do them. They do look better, don't they?

EDWARD (*nodding slightly*): Mmm.

ELIZABETH: He did them all in two days. It's time I did these things. (*Looking about:*) I was thinking of getting a goat.

EDWARD: A goat. What for?

ELIZABETH: I thought she'd keep the grass down in summer. I'd milk her, too. I've seen such similar things in Italy.

EDWARD: Well, yes.

ELIZABETH: In Italy they make cheese with the milk.

EDWARD: You're not going to try that as well?

ELIZABETH: I thought I might, Edward.

EDWARD: But what on earth for? Aren't they a rather beastly, smelly animal? I mean, a goat.

ELIZABETH: Or a pig. I can't eat all the apples.

EDWARD: Please, Aunt, a goat.

ELIZABETH: Two goats.

EDWARD: It's two now.

ELIZABETH: They will be company for one another. Good.

ACT ONE 27

A slight pause.
Bring that young man here soon, Edward.
The lights fade.

Scene Nine

The lights fade up.
A lawn beside Kings College in Cambridge.
Two days later. Monday, October 11th. A warm, autumn sunlight.
VICTOR, in a new suit, is lying on his stomach on the grass. He is surrounded by open textbooks, and he is writing an essay.
EDWARD is some distance away, upside-down, standing on his hands. He has just entered.
EDWARD 'walks' forward. VICTOR hears him and looks up from his essay. When he is a short distance away, EDWARD rights himself.

EDWARD: Isn't it such beautiful weather for October?

VICTOR (*shyly*): Yes.

EDWARD: We haven't been formally introduced. (*Leaning forward, stretching out his hand:*) I'm Edward Longresse.

VICTOR (*stretching forward*): Victor. Victor Ellison.

Their hands can barely stretch the distance, but they manage to shake.

EDWARD: We share the same staircase, you and I.

VICTOR (*shyly*): Yes, I know.

EDWARD feels suddenly shy.

EDWARD: I've asked the porter if he can't mend the stair rail where it's broken. How are you finding Kings?

VICTOR: Well, hard work, at the moment.

EDWARD: I don't seem to have got into the swim of things. I'm not absolutely sure which way to dive.

EDWARD goes red.

VICTOR: There's so much t'do, isn't there?

There is a moment's shyness between them. EDWARD sits.

EDWARD: Why do you work out here on the lawn?

VICTOR: My rooms get stuffy.

EDWARD: Oh yes?

VICTOR: I used to work outside at home.

EDWARD: Where do your people live?

VICTOR: In Yorkshire.

EDWARD: I haven't been to Yorkshire, unfortunately.

EDWARD goes red.

VICTOR: North Yorkshire. Near the Cleveland Hills. Guisborough. It's a little market town, yer know.

EDWARD: My family are in India. In the Punjab.

VICTOR nods.

It's a beastly place. Where the cockroaches scuttle over your food. My father is a lawyer in the Civil Service.

EDWARD goes red.

I hope I'm not sounding like a perfect fool.

VICTOR: No.

EDWARD: I saw a hanging in the Punjab. A coolie was led, handcuffed, through the streets to the gallows. One saw the whites of his eyes through the wet, early morning air. He was a Hindu, held by a man with a fixed bayonet. At eight the bugle called, and the Hindu fell. The doctor present had to pull his legs because he didn't want to die.

VICTOR: That's awful.

EDWARD: I've written an account of it. What is your father?

VICTOR: He's a joiner.

EDWARD: Oh yes?

VICTOR: In Guisborough, yer know.

EDWARD (*smiling*): In Yorkshire?

VICTOR (*smiling*): That's right. Yer get the impression with 'im that he should be doin' more than that.

EDWARD: What do you mean?

VICTOR: If he'd been born like us, he might be here. He left school early.

There is a moment's shyness between them.

EDWARD: You're a music scholar?

VICTOR: Yes.

EDWARD: Is your father musical?

VICTOR: No. I don't know why it suits me. I was encouraged.

EDWARD: So very modest. The provost told me you were a brilliant pianist.

VICTOR (*shrugging*): I don't know.

EDWARD: You're going to play the organ in chapel?

VICTOR: Yes.

There is a moment's shyness between them.

EDWARD: The provost is an old friend of my father's. I had tea with them.

There is a moment's shyness between them.

VICTOR (*smiling*): I find it difficult making friends.

EDWARD (*smiling*): I have been asked to the parties. I've decided not to go.

VICTOR: Why?

EDWARD: It will be like school.

VICTOR: It seems to be a place f' parties – for enjoying yourself. It surprised me. I enjoy working. Are you on a scholarship?

EDWARD: Yes. My family are comfortable, but not rich. My aunt in Middlesex is the one with all the money.

VICTOR: I reckon it's the sort of place you only come to once.

EDWARD *smiles.*

A lot of it's like another language to me. All these toffs. I knew there'd be a few. I'm sorry, I didn't mean you.

EDWARD: Don't apologise, I am a toff.

There is a moment's shyness between them.

Isn't it so superficial? (*After a moment's pause.*) Like you I would like to work hard. It seems important.

VICTOR: I've noticed the light under your door on quite a few nights.

EDWARD: I have a wish to find my own coterie.

There is a moment's shyness between them.

EDWARD *stands up.*

I should leave you if you're working.

They shake hands.
The lights fade.
A slight pause.
The lights fade up.
The wooded coppice at ELIZABETH BRADLEY's *house in Twickenham.*
The following weekend. Sunday, October 17th.
The sky is overcast.
VICTOR *and* EDWARD *are standing on the grass a yard or two apart. They are wearing scarfs.* EDWARD *has an old croquet mallet which he leans on, and swings from side to side, occasionally.*

VICTOR: How did your auntie acquire the house?

EDWARD: My uncle bought it for her. Elizabeth saw it, and fell in love at once.

VICTOR: Is she very rich?

EDWARD: Extremely. She's a millionairess.

VICTOR (*pulling a face*): Really? (*After a moment's pause:*) Phew.

EDWARD: From my Uncle John. She married money. Before the house here in Twickenham, she lived in London. My Uncle John, was the Bradley Bicycle.

VICTOR *pulls a face.*

Have you heard of them?

VICTOR (*interrupting him*): My father has a Bradley. He goes to work on it.

EDWARD: It was the very first safety bicycle. He mass-produced them, and made a fortune. He was an engineer. A thousand accountants run the company now.

VICTOR *nods.*

Uncle John was killed in an aeroplane crash.

VICTOR *pulls a face.*

VICTOR: When?

EDWARD: Six, seven years ago, in the January before the war.

VICTOR (*under his breath*): Phew.

EDWARD: He flew them as his hobby.

VICTOR (*shaking his head*): All this is beyond me.

ACT ONE

EDWARD: I hope I'm not seeming pompous?

VICTOR: No, go on, like.

EDWARD: He was trying to beat the altitude record set by Georges Legagneaux of France. I was in preparatory at the time. Uncle and Aunt were in Tunis in Africa.

VICTOR: What happened?

EDWARD: No one is quite sure. He had to reach over twenty thousand feet..

VICTOR (*under his breath*): Phew.

EDWARD: The wreckage of the aeroplane was eventually found, but Uncle John's body never was. Elizabeth had to spend days while they searched the desert.

VICTOR *nods*.

He was in a Rumpler biplane.

VICTOR: Why were they in Africa?

EDWARD: Because the air is much lighter.

VICTOR: Oh, yes.

EDWARD: Please don't mention aeroplanes to Elizabeth.

VICTOR (*smiling*): I'm frightened of her already.

EDWARD (*smiling*): Why?

VICTOR: The picture you paint.

EDWARD: She takes one by surprise, quite often.

VICTOR (*as much to himself*): I mustn't mention aeroplanes.

EDWARD *smiles*.

EDWARD: Don't worry about her.

VICTOR: I'm not.

VICTOR *wipes his hands on his trousers*.

EDWARD: What are you doing?

VICTOR *mimes shaking hands*.

VICTOR: Getting ready.

EDWARD *laughs*.

If she's an atheist, why's she at church?

EDWARD: It's where she meets her cronies.

VICTOR: Yet she's all this money?

EDWARD: Aunt Elizabeth doesn't flaunt herself.

EDWARD *mimes hitting a croquet ball*.

VICTOR: Has she any children?

EDWARD (*smiling*): Just me.

VICTOR: I meant of her own?

EDWARD: No. I'm more her child than I am my mother's.

VICTOR: She brought you up, Edward?

EDWARD: Yes. I hardly know my own parents. They're little bits of punctuation in a few letters.

VICTOR: Don't they come back?

EDWARD: Every seven years or so.

VICTOR: Isn't that frightening?

EDWARD: Not when it's what you are used to. And her and my mother hardly see eye to eye.

VICTOR: What about?

EDWARD: About me, and about money. My mother's terribly jealous.

VICTOR: Which of them d'you prefer?

EDWARD: Oh, my aunt.

VICTOR *mimes shaking hands. He laughs.* EDWARD *laughs.*
ELIZABETH *enters. She is wearing her best clothes.*

ELIZABETH (*smiling*): Such jollity.

EDWARD: Aunt, this is –

ELIZABETH: Oh, I don't want to know his name, dear. Names spoil everything.

VICTOR *and* ELIZABETH *walk towards each other.*
VICTOR *wipes his hand on his trousers.*
They shake hands.

VICTOR: Edward was telling me about aeroplanes.

ELIZABETH *laughs. She walks away a few paces. She turns.*

ELIZABETH: And Edward told you not to mention them?

VICTOR (*looking down slightly*): Yes, I'm sorry.

ELIZABETH (*smiling*): It is so lovely to meet his friends.

VICTOR (*shyly*): Thank you for having me for the day.

ELIZABETH: We will have luncheon. And then you shall play the piano.

VICTOR: Yes.

ELIZABETH: And I have some pieces I would like explained. By Schubert.

VICTOR: I'll try.

ELIZABETH: No, dear, you will succeed.

VICTOR *looks at* EDWARD.

VICTOR (*going to* ELIZABETH): Mrs Bradley, I think we've got off on the wrong foot.

ELIZABETH: I will listen to you and see.

VICTOR: Edward didn't tell me you were interested in music.

ELIZABETH: I have an amateur appreciation.

VICTOR: That is all I have.

ELIZABETH: Then why are you at Kings?

VICTOR *doesn't know what to say*.

Dear, I do so hate modesty. We will go to lunch.

ELIZABETH *links her arm through* VICTOR's. *They go out followed by* EDWARD.

The lights fade.

Scene Ten

The lights fade up.
The wooded coppice. There is a deckchair.
Three years later. Tuesday, May 1st 1923. A bright sun is shining.
VICTOR *and* EDWARD *are in shirt sleeves. They are standing on their heads.*

VICTOR: Two hundred and twenty-three.

EDWARD: Two hundred and twenty-four.

VICTOR: Two hundred and twenty-five.

EDWARD: Two hundred and twenty-six.

VICTOR: Two hundred and twenty-seven.

EDWARD: Two hundred and twenty-eight.

EDWARD *topples over*. VICTOR *quickly follows*.

(*Dreamily:*) That was by far the longest.

VICTOR *and* EDWARD *lie back. They are panting slightly. They look at the sky. Silence.*

What are you thinking about?

Silence.

Aren't we egoists?

Silence.

VICTOR (*dreamily*): You are, Edward.

EDWARD: You, too.

A slight pause.

VICTOR: What were you thinking?

EDWARD: That I hardly knew you.

A slight pause.

If we were queer, we could make love to one another.

VICTOR: I used to think you were.

EDWARD: So did I. I hoped. Wouldn't it have been wonderfully romantic?

A slight pause.

At Eton there were little liaisons in every corridor.

VICTOR *crawls on his elbows closer to* EDWARD.

VICTOR: Did you?

EDWARD: Once or twice.

VICTOR: Who with?

EDWARD: He's in the House of Lords. He was an Oppidan.

A slight pause.

Will I make a writer, Victor?

VICTOR: I don't know.

A slight pause.

I thought you wanted to be a politician.

EDWARD: Both. I can be a socialist and a writer.

VICTOR: No, you can't.

EDWARD *rolls onto his stomach. They are lying in a straight line, looking at one another.*

EDWARD: One must actually write in a socialist way.

VICTOR: How d'you do that?

ACT ONE 31

EDWARD: By understanding people and facing issues.

VICTOR: That's what every artist does.

EDWARD: By facing unpleasant facts.

VICTOR: You're in a privileged position.

EDWARD: Are you going to feel guilty all your life?

A slight pause.

VICTOR: An artist can't have politics. He has to be free.

EDWARD: You're behind the times.

A slight pause.

VICTOR: Maybe.

A slight pause.

All art is arrogance.

EDWARD: All good art.

A slight pause.

VICTOR: I should have told you, Edward, I've applied for a job.

A slight pause.

No, to be honest I've got the job.

EDWARD: Where?

VICTOR: At my old grammar school. Teaching music and maths.

EDWARD: What for?

VICTOR: I've a living to make.

EDWARD: Starve.

VICTOR: You are a romantic. I hadn't realised.

A slight pause.

EDWARD: As a matter of fact, I've done the same.

VICTOR: At Eton?

EDWARD: No, my old preparatory.

VICTOR: Teaching?

EDWARD: Washing up, Victor. (*After a moment's pause*:) Teaching everything.

VICTOR: Why haven't we told each other?

EDWARD: Have you a cigarette?

VICTOR: We smoked the last.

EDWARD: Go to the house for some.

VICTOR: You go. (*After a moment's pause:*) Call Pickles.

A slight pause.

EDWARD: Why do you fight your intellect, Victor? What are you frightened of?

VICTOR: I wish I'd been warned about your charm. And your arrogant self-confidence.

EDWARD: But not self-congratulation. There's a difference.

VICTOR: Is there?

EDWARD: A fine one, admittedly. The difference between genius in confidence and mediocrity in congratulation.

VICTOR: You're too clever for your own good.

EDWARD *rolls onto his back. He looks at the sky.*

EDWARD: A man cannot afford to have doubt. We have to know that socialism is right.

VICTOR: That's just where you're wrong.

EDWARD (*after a moment's pause*): Don't you want the world to change?

VICTOR: You misinterpret everything I say. (*After a moment's pause*:) To be fair, I don't know.

A slight pause.

EDWARD: I was right, you are frightened.

VICTOR (*slightly annoyed*): You say everything from a position of comfort.

EDWARD: I accept that. For the moment. It is largely not my fault. (*Rolling onto his side*:) And actually, I do have doubts.

EDWARD *leans on his elbow.*

I have doubts about my own ability to make sense of what I see.

VICTOR: So do I. That's all I'm saying. The difference between us is one of class. One of assumption. I don't presume, Edward.

EDWARD: I'm sorry, I didn't meant to offend you.

VICTOR: You haven't.

Silence.

You know who I think about most? My mother.

Silence.

The mother who died when my sister was born. I hated her.

EDWARD: Your mother or your sister?

VICTOR: Lucy, my little sister. I was seventeen, taking my exams. I've grown to like her in the hols. Isn't that funny?

EDWARD (*after a moment's pause*): Have you spoken to your father?

VICTOR: I wouldn't ever – not about that.

EDWARD: It's perfectly natural.

VICTOR: Is it?

EDWARD: I've a book by Sigmund Freud.

VICTOR (*annoyed*): Oh shut up, Edward.

ELIZABETH *enters*.

ELIZABETH: Edward, be a dear, and go up the house and collect the tea things.

EDWARD: I can take a hint.

EDWARD *jumps up*.

VICTOR (*picking himself up*): I can go.

ELIZABETH: Edward knows I wish to speak to you on a personal matter.

EDWARD *exits*.

VICTOR (*calling after him*): Bring some cigarettes.

ELIZABETH *is looking at* VICTOR.
VICTOR *takes a cigarette packet from his trouser pocket. He looks inside, it is empty. He puts the packet back in his trouser pocket.*
ELIZABETH *sits in the deckchair.*

What is it, Elizabeth?

ELIZABETH: Edward's a funny boy, don't you think?

VICTOR: Yes, I suppose so.

ELIZABETH: Full, these days, of a peculiar sureness. I would say it was haughty, but I don't think it is. No. That wouldn't quite be the truth. Don't we often express the opposite of what we truly feel, Victor?

VICTOR: Sometimes, yes.

ELIZABETH (*wondering herself*): I wonder why that is? (*Seeing the answer. Brightly:*) Fear, perhaps? The fear of being alone? The fear of (*Searching for the words:*) standing out.

A slight pause.

No, Edward does have doubt. He needs a little more. He has to find his own way in the world. (*Smiling:*) You, I'm not sure. The world may destroy your talent before it's even born.

VICTOR: I don't understand.

ELIZABETH: Edward is a willow-o'-the-wisp. I think – I think, Victor – that you are not.

VICTOR *looks down slightly.*

Edward has declined my help. I'm sure with good reason. You, I've no doubt, should accept it.

VICTOR *looks up.*

I have no wish for, nor do I expect, your gratitude.

VICTOR *walks a few paces.*

Isn't it funny, Victor, after all this time I still don't feel I know you. Edward is all too obvious. That is why he will never be the great writer. And this socialist nonsense. He knows that, I believe.

VICTOR *opens his mouth to contradict her.*

Saying that has nothing to do with the love that I feel for him.

A slight pause.

I don't know if you will ever truly love anyone, Victor. I don't know what it is. There's something about you. A meanness of spirit.

VICTOR: Will Edward love?

ELIZABETH: Oh, I think so. Quite soon.

VICTOR: You're being very blunt.

ELIZABETH: Yes, I meant to be, as a matter of fact.

VICTOR: What is it that you want?

ELIZABETH: Quite simply, I'd like the honour of helping you.

VICTOR: Would it be an honour?

ELIZABETH (*thinking*): Yes, I don't like you, Victor. Isn't that strange?

VICTOR: Yes, it is.

ELIZABETH: I once told Edward he had to learn to like himself. That's a hard lesson.

A slight pause.

ACT ONE 33

I had in mind a yearly allowance. If we said fifteen hundred to begin with.

VICTOR (*not sure what to say*): That's more than I could ever dream of.

ELIZABETH (*heartfelt*): I would so like you to dream.

VICTOR: I'd never thought of having a patron.

ELIZABETH: Dreams make our world. How can we dream if we have no money. It will give you a freedom.

VICTOR: Why me, Elizabeth?

ELIZABETH: Yours is a special talent. I want to hear that perfection in your music.

A slight pause.

I don't have to see you. Go abroad. Go anywhere. (*Excited:*) I don't want to see you. We might loathe each other. I want to hear your life in your music. I want to hear your soul.

VICTOR: Have I a soul?

A slight pause.

ELIZABETH: So little faith, Victor.

A slight pause.

You are not perfect, but your music can be.

VICTOR *walks a few paces.*

(*Heartfelt*:) Compose for me. Please. Please.

VICTOR: I can't, Elizabeth, you know that.

ELIZABETH: I was afraid.

A slight pause.

I'm sorry.

A slight pause.
Sudden blackout.

Scene Eleven

The lights are snapped up.
A lawn beside a road in Cambridge.
There is a postbox on the pavement.
A few days later. Saturday, May 5th.
A bright sun is shining.
DOROTHY is lying on the grass. She is wearing a summer dress and she is reading a book.
A pause.
VICTOR enters. He has a pile of books under his arm, and a letter in his other hand. He walks to the postbox and looks at the collection times.

VICTOR: Excuse me.

DOROTHY *looks up from her book.*

Has the post been collected yet?

DOROTHY: I haven't noticed.

VICTOR *posts his letter. He exits.*
DOROTHY goes back to her book.
A pause.
Sudden blackout.

ACT TWO

Scene One

From the darkness a song. VICTOR sings the tune, WILFRED a harmony.

A Song

Loud we mourned him aloft we've borne him,
Our young brigadier when we found him,
In the ground we gently laid him,
We beat our drum then we mourned no more,
In his mouth there was music ringing,
At Cerro Rojo with the bullets round him,
Come the stuka from heaven singing,
Muffle your drum for my love sings no more.

On my bed where I lay weeping
On my bed there is no resting
Many nights now without sleeping
Thoughts of my love go tumbling round.
Dream I see him see him coming
In the clouds I see him standing
Jimmy there in his bloody shroud.

The words are by Martin Carthy to the tune of 'Lord Byron'.
The lights have travelled up during the song.
The platform of a railway station somewhere in the wilds of Spain between Albacete and Villarrubia de Santiago. (In the original production the station was identified as Morata.)
Early February, 1937.
Night. A moon is shining.
There is a collection of English men on the platform, all are awake but all are trying to catch sleep. They are lying on whatever they can find, and all are wearing the rough 'Uniform' of The International Brigade.
VICTOR ELLISON and WILFRED FOX are side by side.
ERNEST HURLL is on his own.
ERNEST is RICHARD's twin brother and looks identical to him.
PETER DEAN is on his own. He is sitting on a bench. PETER was born in 1905. He is a thin wiry, cultured-looking man with receding hair. There is a shyness and gentleness about him, but his voice is neither refined nor soft.
HEINZ BAYER is standing on his own. He has just entered. He has listened to the song.
HEINZ was born in 1910. He is a German. There is something proud, but not arrogant, about the way he stands and conducts himself. He is blonde haired and clean faced.
HEINZ goes first to VICTOR and WILFRED.

HEINZ: You are English? You have a cigarette for me?

VICTOR: No, sorry. Have you, Wilf?

WILFRED: Smoked 'em.

HEINZ goes to ERNEST.

HEINZ: You are English? You have a cigarette for me?

ERNEST: I don't smoke.

HEINZ: That is rare for an Englishman, Comrade.

HEINZ goes towards PETER. PETER takes a packet of Spanish cigarettes from his pocket. He gives them to HEINZ. HEINZ opens the packet.

But it is your last one?

PETER: Then it doesn't matter.

HEINZ: Thank you. You are a friend.

HEINZ lights the cigarette with an old lighter.

PETER: Where are you from?

HEINZ: Of course, from Germany.

PETER: Your English is very good.

HEINZ: Of course, but why not?

PETER: No reason.

HEINZ (*sitting down beside PETER on the bench*): I learn my English because I am very clever at school. The top of my class, always. I read your Dickens, and your Thomas Hardy. You speak German, my friend?

PETER: No.

HEINZ: But why is this? This is not good.

PETER (*smiling*): I was always bottom of my class.

HEINZ: This I do not believe. (*Holding the cigarette up:*) This cigarette is proof of generosity.

ACT TWO   35

PETER: I don't understand?

HEINZ: You are here in Spain. You were top of the class. If not then, now.

PETER: Being generous doesn't make you clever.

HEINZ: Oh, but I think so, no? (*To them all:*) *The Mayor of Casterbridge*, is a great book.

PETER *looks puzzled.*

You do not read, I can tell. We talk about something else.

PETER *changes position, he gets more comfortable.*

PETER: Whereabouts in Germany are you from?

HEINZ: Berlin. Our greatest city. You know Berlin?

PETER (*shaking his head*): No.

HEINZ: That is a pity, my friend. I love Germany. (*Offering* PETER *the cigarette:*) You wish to inhale?

PETER: No.

HEINZ: Then I steal it all, I do not care. I steal all the time at home in Berlin. It is my life, this begging. (*Holding the cigarette up:*) Where you get this Spanish cigarette?

PETER: A lady put them in my pocket in Albacete.

WILFRED: She gave me a packet.

HEINZ: They are grateful to us, my friends. I get oranges one day. She does not know you do not smoke?

PETER (*smiling*): No. I would have preferred a bottle of wine.

HEINZ: The Manchegan wine it is beautiful here. Like the cheese. The peasants they chill it in the mountain streams. It is the way to be drunk.

PETER: How long have you been in Spain?

HEINZ: I come here to fight, Comrade. And you?

PETER: Seven weeks.

HEINZ: At your training camp?

PETER: Yes.

HEINZ: Now you go to the front?

PETER: When our next train arrives.

HEINZ: It is not to be frightened, my friend.

The sound of an aeroplane, high, and in the distance.

The men prick up their ears, they listen.

VICTOR (*to* WILFRED): Whose is it?

WILFRED: I don't know.

HEINZ: It is a German aeroplane. The enemy. I can tell by his purr. Sadly, we do not see eye to eye.

A slight pause.

He is stupid. He do not know where we are. I am the one with the eyes of a cat.

The aeroplane goes.
Silence.
The men relax.

PETER: How did you get here?

HEINZ: Of course on a boat from Hamburg. I stow away like Jim in a book called *Treasure Island*. I see the aeroplanes, these weapons. It is dangerous for me. Then when I am here I cross the enemy lines like Jesus, on a donkey.

A moment's pause.

In Berlin I am a prostitute, my friends. My family is very poor. I, the eldest. My father is sick from his work in the glass factory. There are seven children, seven of us and no food. I find the ways and the means. It is dangerous now in Berlin, to be a prostitute. It is dangerous now in Berlin everywhere. The police they raid the Cosy Corner Café. I am a lucky one.

HEINZ *looks between them.*

Of course with other men.

A moment's pause.

One quarter of Berlin is full of boys waiting. Me, I have two. My rich German banker, my English writer. He, he has poverty, but I persuade him. My banker is a Jew, with a big house in the country by a lake. His wife, she does not know. We have to be very secretive together. My writer is very jealous of this relationship. I tell him it end, then he empty his pockets for me. I tell him it end, many times. He always nearly trust me. My writer will be famous one day. His parents they send him more money.

HEINZ *looks between them.*
But why are you shocked? You have poverty in England? My brothers they go through school this way.

A slight pause.

I think it is better we speak the truth about ourselves. We are comrades here. This is the way we should learn. We do not only fight with a rifle, my friends. In this war we are fighting for the truth. It is why we are here. The truth is in our souls.

A slight pause.

My fat German banker, he is taken by a jackboot. The interrogation it leave a scar. He take his family with him when he go. My English writer also flee this country. My brother, he is fourteen, in his uniform. He goosestep like a pimpernel. He tell the authorities about me. You English, you have no imagination. You do not know about Europe. Only yourselves. Soon, there will be a war. This is why we must win Spain. Herr Hitler he flex his muscles.

A slight pause.

VICTOR: Yes.

HEINZ: This fascism, it is not inevitable. But difficult. It take strong men. And we are strong.

A slight pause.

VICTOR: What is happening to your family?

HEINZ: Herr Hitler he is offering hope, Comrade. You, you punish Germany too much in 1918. We look for our pride. (*To* PETER:) I say to you a moment ago, that generosity make you clever. The English would have been clever to be generous. (*Looking between them*:) Sadly, not so.

A slight pause.

ERNEST: Me'be we had our pride an' all like. I lost me dad. Me mam had to bring us up on nothin', yer know.

A slight pause.

We could all go round faulting other folk.

HEINZ (*gently*): I understand, my friend.

ERNEST: Yer have to be responsible for yourself, I reckon.

HEINZ (*looking between them*): Which is why we are here. (*To* ERNEST:) Are you married, Comrade?

ERNEST: What's that got to do with owt?

HEINZ: I speak to you as a friend. I am not, as you say, homosexual. My writer, he is very.

ERNEST: Aye, sorry. No, like.

HEINZ (*to* PETER): You?

PETER: No.

HEINZ (*to* VICTOR): You?

VICTOR: Yes. And a girlfriend.

HEINZ (*to* WILFRED): You?

WILFRED: Yes.

HEINZ: A girlfriend also?

WILFRED: I leave that sort of thing up to him.

HEINZ (*looking between them*): And where do you come from?

VICTOR: Guisborough.

WILFRED: Guisborough.

ERNEST: Newcastle.

PETER: Manchester.

HEINZ (*smiling*): I wish I was wiser. My writer, he is from public school. They call it Chatterhouse. Of course, he hate it very much. He teach English in Berlin to the hatted ladies.

HEINZ *blows into his hands.*

It is cold.

HEINZ *changes position, he gets more comfortable.*

PETER: This train doesn't want to come.

HEINZ: It does not, my friend. The trains here they are like a tortoise. (*After a moment's pause:*) May I ask what you do in Manchester?

PETER: I'm an entertainer.

HEINZ: Ah. I see.

PETER: I'm a stage artiste in the variety theatres.

HEINZ (*interested*): This is something I have not heard. With my writer we go to the opera.

PETER: I've an act which I do.

HEINZ: An act?

PETER *opens his case. He takes out a boy ventriloquist's doll. It looks very much like him.*

ACT TWO   37

PETER: I work with this thing. He's called Johnnie.

JOHNNIE (*coming to life*): Hello.

HEINZ: Hello, Johnnie. How do you do?

JOHNNIE *looks at* PETER, *and then back to* HEINZ.

JOHNNIE: I was the trade unionist in a cycle factory.

PETER: A trade unionist in a cycle factory?

JOHNNIE: I was the spokesman.

JOHNNIE *laughs.*

PETER: Don't be silly. Tell the truth. Johnnie goes to school, don't you?

JOHNNIE: I'm cleverer than him.

PETER: Now don't show off.

JOHNNIE: Why?

PETER: Because it's insulting to be bigheaded.

JOHNNIE: He can't read, you know.

PETER: Stop it, Johnnie.

JOHNNIE: I have to read to him. Don't I?

WILFRED: Where did you learn that?

JOHNNIE (*straining to look*): Did he say something over there?

PETER: Johnnie, come here.

JOHNNIE: I was't learnt, I was conceived, just like you – on a drunken Friday night.

PETER: Ignore him.

WILFRED (*mystified*): I don't know who I'm talking to.

JOHNNIE: Yer talkin' t'me, yer fool. Yer talkin' to a bit of wood.

WILFRED: I'll come over there and saw you in half.

JOHNNIE: Magician, are you?

PETER: Johnnie.

JOHNNIE: What?

PETER: Stop it.

JOHNNIE: He started it.

PETER: Stop it.

JOHNNIE: Why?

PETER: Because it's rude.

JOHNNIE: He was rude first.

PETER: That's not the point.

JOHNNIE (*resting his head on* PETER*'s shoulder*): He said he'd saw me in half. I don't want sawing.

PETER (*to* WILFRED): Please say you didn't mean it. He'll never go to bed.

WILFRED (*confused*): I didn't mean it.

PETER (*turning his head to* WILFRED): Thank you.

The doll goes limp.

ERNEST: Where did yer learn that like?

PETER: My father was a vent. Johnnie was one of his dolls.

ERNEST: How long have yer been doing it?

PETER: Since I was twelve.

JOHNNIE (*coming to life*): My age?

PETER: That's right. Go to sleep.

JOHNNIE (*resting his head on* PETER*'s shoulder*): Will I be a vent when I grow up?

PETER: Yes.

JOHNNIE: Can I have a glass of water?

PETER: You'll wet the bed.

JOHNNIE: I won't.

PETER: You will.

JOHNNIE: Won't.

PETER: I'll take you to bits.

JOHNNIE: Wouldn't dare.

PETER *pulls off one of* JOHNNIE*'s legs.* JOHNNIE *looks down to where it used to be. He looks back to* PETER.

Ow.

PETER: You can have it back in the morning.

JOHNNIE: Is that so I won't come downstairs?

PETER (*taking* JOHNNIE*'s other leg off*): Yes.

JOHNNIE: Ow. What d'you call a man with no legs?

PETER: I don't know. What do you call a man with no legs?

JOHNNIE: A low down bum.

JOHNNIE *laughs.*

PETER: Johnnie.

JOHNNIE: What?

PETER: Close your eyes and go to sleep.

JOHNNIE rests his head on PETER's shoulder.

Better?

JOHNNIE: Yes.

PETER: Sweet dreams.

JOHNNIE: Yes.

A slight pause.

Eh, I haven't had me read, you, read me a story.

The sound of an aeroplane, high, and in the distance.
The men prick up their ears, they look and listen. JOHNNIE *looks too.*

VICTOR (*to* HEINZ): Whose is that?

HEINZ: Germany again.

A slight pause.
The aeroplane goes.
The men relax.
JOHNNIE *goes to sleep on* PETER's *shoulder. Without the doll* PETER *becomes shy again.*

I find this very interesting. He seem to have a life of his own.

PETER: I get tired of him sometimes.

HEINZ: But your hand it work him?

PETER: Yes.

HEINZ: Explain please.

PETER: I'd like him to grow up. He never does. He's always the same.

HEINZ: You could get another doll, no?

PETER: The audience won't let me.

HEINZ: But why?

PETER: An audience likes what it feels comfortable with. I've two acts, I've been doing them for ten years, in the same theatres.

HEINZ *nods.*

VICTOR: Where d'you work?

PETER: Lancashire. The West Riding. Mainly.

HEINZ: You bring him all this way?

PETER: I couldn't leave him at home. (*Smiling*:) We walked across the Pyrenees together. He'll die with me, if we do.

HEINZ: Why do you both come to Spain?

PETER: We're communists. Or I am. He's nothing.

HEINZ: I find you surprising.

PETER: Why?

HEINZ: But I like to be surprised. Karl Marx, he was a German.

PETER: Yes.

HEINZ: He is buried in your London.

PETER: Yes, I know. My father met him.

HEINZ: Your father, he was a communist?

PETER: He didn't know he was. He would be, if he were alive.

VICTOR: Did he?

PETER: Yes.

VICTOR: How?

PETER: He wrote to him. They met in a café.

VICTOR: When?

PETER: Years and years ago. He was a very young man. Marx was frail.

HEINZ: Your father was converted?

PETER: My father was a natural communist. He didn't have an ideology. He didn't give names to things. I do.

HEINZ: My friend, I am not a communist, I have a soul. You understand?

PETER: What d'you mean by the soul?

HEINZ: I mean the mysteries of myself. The things in me that I do not understand. We all have those things. Everyday we change a little bit more and it make us think again. Communism, it deny these mysteries. (*Smiling*:) I like to have them. It make me human.

PETER: D'you believe in God?

HEINZ: Comrade, nearly, yes.

PETER: We both believe in human potential, don't we? The church is an instrument of represssion.

HEINZ (*struggling*): You will have to go more slowly. It is hard for me to talk of philosophy in another language.

PETER: I'm sorry.

HEINZ: Please?

PETER (*slowly*): I have sat in churches where the gentry looked down on the peasant.

HEINZ: That for me is not the church. I want a new church.

PETER: No, that is the church.

HEINZ: Then I change it by myself. God is the mystery for me. I like Him.

PETER: The ceremonies of the church deny an individual separate thought.

HEINZ: The ceremony of the church is the human expression of God, no?

PETER (*shaking his head*): No.

HEINZ: But it is.

PETER: No, it's worship.

HEINZ: We are very the same, you and me. I have a different view of God. My view of God will make things right for all people. I am not a communist. I believe in liberty. But I have a soul. It is for my soul that I am here. Jesus, he was a fighter. He overturn the tables of the money lenders.

VICTOR, WILFRED *and* ERNEST *have been listening.*
There is a short silence.

(*Smiling:*) Johnnie he has gone to sleep?

PETER (*smiling*): Yes.

HEINZ: Your father, he is an interesting man?

PETER: Yes.

HEINZ: Johnnie say you cannot read, no? Is that the truth about you?

PETER: Yes.

HEINZ: I thought so. Something tell me.

PETER: I've tried many times. I just can't do it.

HEINZ (*smiling*): I read too much with my English writer.

PETER *smiles.*
A short silence.
ERNEST *stands up.*

ERNEST: Are you a Catholic?

HEINZ: Not yet, my friend.

ERNEST *joins them, he sits down on the bench.*

But nearly. I look into it. My writer, he is a Catholic. You are from Newcastle?

ERNEST (*getting comfortable*): Yes.

HEINZ: Good, I remember. Comrades, I will tell you why so nearly a Catholic. It is to do with love. If we hate a man and he dies, our hatred dies quickly with him, it is soon forgotten. If we love someone, our love it live on and grow through the years. (*Looking at the sky.*) It is Him up there. He load the dice that way.

ERNEST: I'm a Catholic, yer know.

HEINZ: Then we talk you and me. Catholics are turbulent people.

ERNEST: Isn't prostitution a sin?

HEINZ: We are above that here in Spain. It is for a bigger cause we fight. Jesus, he sat with prostitutes.

ERNEST: Try the Church of England.

HEINZ (*smiling, gripping* ERNEST's *knee*): My friend, you make me laugh.

ERNEST: I just wanted to know like.

HEINZ: Because, my friend, I am ignorant. I feel somewhere there is a faith, that is all. I try and go towards it.

ERNEST: That's all right like.

HEINZ: Newcastle, Newcastle?

ERNEST: It's the north east.

HEINZ: That is nowhere near Chatterhouse?

ERNEST: I wouldn't know.

HEINZ: You too walk over the mountains?

ERNEST: Not together like. Not with Peter. I came on me own, without this lot.

VICTOR *stands up.*

HEINZ: You walk too?

VICTOR: Yes.

VICTOR *sits with them on the bench.*

If anyone asks we're in Paris. Beneath the Eiffel Tower. Sipping champagne.

HEINZ: My friend, you joke with me?

VICTOR: Only partly.

ERNEST: It's the way we all got here like, on a weekend trip to Paris.

HEINZ: Yes? (*To* VICTOR:) You also?

VICTOR: Then down through France by train and across the frontier.

HEINZ (*smiling*): We go and borrow a train, no?

HEINZ blows into his hands.
It is cold on this station.

WILFRED stands up.
You join us too, my friend?

WILFRED sits with them, on the ground.
I am glad I came for the cigarette.

WILFRED takes a packet of cigarettes from his pocket.
HEINZ looks at him.

WILFRED: Yeh, 'a lied. Sorry.

WILFRED offers the cigarettes. VICTOR and HEINZ take one. HEINZ lights them with his lighter.
They smoke in silence for a moment.

VICTOR: Luxury.

WILFRED: Aye.

HEINZ: I smoke so little, it make me strange.

PETER: Can I have one?

WILFRED gives him a cigarette. HEINZ lights it. PETER hasn't smoked before.

ERNEST: I keep wonderin' what day it is. Or what month even, yer know.

WILFRED: February.

ERNEST: Yer sure?

WILFRED: Aye. Tuesday.

A slight pause.

Or Wednesday. Thursday. One of those. (*After a moment's pause:*) Monday me'be. Saturday. (*After a moment's pause:*) Friday.

VICTOR: There's only Sunday left, Wilf.

WILFRED: No, it's definitely not Sunday.

They smile.

ERNEST: Can I have one, please?

WILFRED gives ERNEST a cigarette.
PETER gives him his cigarette to light it from.
They smoke.

PETER: If this train comes.

ERNEST coughs.

WILFRED: Give us it 'ere.

ERNEST gives WILFRED the cigarette. WILFRED puts the two cigarettes together between his fingers, he smokes them both. ERNEST is still coughing.

ERNEST (*red in the face*): It's bloody awful.

PETER (*to* VICTOR): D'you want this one?

VICTOR takes it. He puts it out on the soul of his boot and keeps it.
They smoke.

ERNEST (*to* WILFRED): I wonder how our lad is?

HEINZ (*not understanding*): What is your lad?

ERNEST: Me brother like, yer know. Me twin, in Newcastle.

WILFRED: All right, I should think, he's got my bike.

ERNEST: I've written to him. Don't know if it'll get there.

WILFRED: It will.

ERNEST: Yer reckon?

WILFRED: Yeh, a certainty.

ERNEST: I don't have your confidence

WILFRED: Why not?

ERNEST (*shrugging*): Don't know. (*After a moment's pause:*) It's a bloody long way to the north east.

WILFRED: D'yer miss 'im?

ERNEST: Sometimes, yes. (*After a moment's pause:*) I must have been mad to set off here.

ERNEST smiles.
Silence.
WILFRED puts the two cigarettes up his nose, one up each nostril.

ACT TWO 41

The men smile.
WILFRED *takes them out. He smokes.*
Silence.

WILFRED (*the first time he has said these things*): I don't think I was mad. I came here for the future. If you can't see a future, what can yer see? Nothing. It's the possibility of what might be, that makes your life what it is.

A slight pause.

If you can't see anything, what have you? You might as well curl up and die.

HEINZ: It is the same for all of us here.

The sound of a train. It pulls into the station. Steam from the engine billows out. The five men stand up.
Sudden blackout.

Scene Two

The lights are snapped up.
'Suicide Hill' on the front line at Jarama.
An open plateau. There are two separate defence shields which have been built very quickly from dry stone: they are little more than mounds, but are roughly in the shape of small shooting-butts. The air in front is smokey, as if the soldiers behind the butts were looking into an infinity.
A few days later. Late afternoon.
PETER and HEINZ are behind one butt, VICTOR and ERNEST, behind the other. Each has a rifle.
A loud rifle-fire, and some automatic-fire, is ringing out from the enemy a few hundred yards away.
The four soldiers are well down in their butts.
A slight pause.
VICTOR raises his rifle. He shoots over the butt. PETER, in his butt, does the same. When they have let off their shots, they quickly duck down again. PETER and VICTOR begin to reload.
A slight pause.
The enemy fire dies to silence.

VICTOR: There's a bastard keeps shooting at me.

PETER: We're out-numbered.

VICTOR: How're we meant to move forward?

Enemy rifle-fire rings out. ERNEST *and* HEINZ *make a move: it is their turn to shoot.*

Wait till they reload. (*Shouting across to* HEINZ *in the other butt:*) Heinz, wait till they reload.

ERNEST *and* HEINZ *stay down.*

HEINZ (*calling back*): We will not see them then. They will be down like us. We shoot when they shoot.

VICTOR: No. Wait. This way we get the first shots.

HEINZ: They have automatic weapons. (*Holding up his rifle:*) This, this is a hundred years old. It kill me first.

A slight pause.

ERNEST: This is hopeless.

VICTOR: I know.

The enemy fire slowly dies to silence. The silence is almost eerie.
A slight pause.

Right, Comrades.

ERNEST, VICTOR *and* PETER *raise their rifles over their respective butts.*
A moment's pause.

All right, Heinz?

HEINZ (*raising his rifle*): Yes, my friend.

VICTOR: Wait until they come up, and you've a clear view. I want them to think we're falling back.

The four soldiers wait, their fingers poised on the triggers of their rifles.

HEINZ: This is the dangerous way, Comrades, they get a chance to see us.

PETER: It's better than firing at nothing.

A slight pause.

VICTOR: Where the hell are they?

A slight pause.

HEINZ: Franco, he put them to sleep with his charm.

A slight pause.

I like a joke from Johnnie, at this time.

PETER: I left him in the cookhouse.

HEINZ: I hope he do not eat all our food. These beans and olive oil. It make him go to the toilet all the time, like us, no?

A pause.

ERNEST: Me'be they've retreated like.

A pause.

HEINZ (*intense*): I have one, Comrades. The top of his head. They think we have gone back into the olive groves.

VICTOR: Wait until you can see him more clearly.

HEINZ (*intense*): They will see us if we wait too long.

A slight pause.

Yes, they are beginning to move.

VICTOR: Got them?

PETER: Yes.

ERNEST: Yeh.

A slight pause.

VICTOR: Let them come a bit more, let them come a bit more.

A slight pause.

HEINZ: They are thinking we are cowards. One, he has lit a cigarette.

A slight pause.

(*Really intense:*) Yes, now I see him smoking.

A slight pause.

VICTOR: Wait.

A slight pause.

Wait.

A slight pause.

Wait.

HEINZ *fires first. The other three soldiers follow quickly with their shots. They duck down, behind the butts, immediately.*

PETER: Get him?

HEINZ (*smiling*): I think so, my friend. Where is their answer to that?

HEINZ *raises his head to peer above the butt.*

A single rifle-shot rings out from the enemy.

HEINZ *is hit in the neck. The force of the shot pushes him away from the butt.*

A massive round of continuous fire rings out from the enemy.

PETER *makes a move to help* HEINZ.

VICTOR (*reloading. Screaming*): Leave him.

The soldiers stay down in their butts, VICTOR *and* ERNEST *still reloading.*

PETER (*screaming*): Heinz. Heinz.

HEINZ (*very slightly raising his head*): I am all right, my friend, it is not bad.

HEINZ *starts to crawl towards* PETER's *butt.*

Enemy fire is still ringing out.

VICTOR *drops his rifle. He rushes to* HEINZ. *He helps drag him,* HEINZ *trying to stand, to the butt where* PETER *is. They make it. They get down.* HEINZ *has his head on* VICTOR's *lap.*

Thank you, my friend. Where am I hit?

VICTOR (*looking at him*): In the neck.

Blood is pouring from HEINZ's *wound.*

HEINZ: The fascists have me, haven't they?

VICTOR (*gently*): No.

HEINZ: My friend, you are a bad liar. It does you credit.

Enemy fire is still ringing out.
In the other butt ERNEST *raises his rifle. He fires the single shot. He ducks down and starts to reload.*

Once, in the slums of Berlin, I see a young boy. He is naked and bleeding from the ruins of his life.

PETER (*gently*): Quiet.

HEINZ: I watch him being clothed, in the false clothes of lies. And as he grows up he becomes proud, the pride of deceit. He is led along this road by inaction and fear. When he is given a bomb, he will drop it wherever he is told. My friends, the bombs will fall on Europe. We are not enough. (*Proudly:*) Though our pride is right. (*Shivering:*) I am cold, so very cold. (*Looking at* VICTOR:) God, he will forgive me, yes?

VICTOR: Yes.

HEINZ: Please, if you would give me absolution from my sins.

VICTOR (*gently*): I don't know how you do that.

ACT TWO

HEINZ: A prayer will do, please.

PETER (*gently*): You're not going to die.

HEINZ (*smiling. Blood coming from his mouth*): But of course not. The prayer is for you, my friends.

PETER *looks at* VICTOR.

VICTOR: O God, the Father of our Lord Jesus Christ, our Only Saviour, the Prince of Peace: Give us grace seriously to lay to heart the great dangers we are in by our unhappy divisions. Take away all hatred and prejudice, and whatsoever else may hinder us from Godly union and concord:

Enemy fire is still ringing out.
In the other butt ERNEST *raises his rifle. He fires the single shot. He ducks down and starts to reload.*

that, as there is but one Body, and one Spirit, and one Hope of our calling, one Lord, one Faith, one Baptism, one God and Father of us all, so we henceforth be all of one heart, and of one soul, united in one holy bond of Truth and Peace, of Faith and Charity, and may with one mind and one mouth glorify thee today: through Jesus Christ our Lord. Amen.

HEINZ: That is very good. Only a little bit false.

PETER *looks at* VICTOR.

VICTOR (*shrugging*): My headmaster says it.

WILFRED *enters running, ducking low. He has a pistol. He fires. He joins* EARNEST.

WILFRED (*shouting*): The command is to pull back beyond the sunken road. We're heavily out-numbered.

PETER: How many are hit?

WILFRED: Quite a few. It's chaos.

A slight pause.

VICTOR: We'd better prepare to fall back then. Heinz is hit. We need a stretcher.

HEINZ *has his eyes closed.*

PETER (*looking at him*): He's dead. (*Gently pulling* HEINZ's *arm*:) Heinz.

VICTOR *looks at* HEINZ.

WILFRED: Is he all right?

VICTOR (*calling back*): No, we think he's dead.

VICTOR *takes off his jacket. His shirt, by his right shoulder, is soaked in blood.*

PETER: When did you get that?

VICTOR (*wincing with pain*): When I helped him.

The enemy fire has stopped: it has ended with one last single shot.
Silence for a moment.
PETER *takes a rag from his pocket, he starts to dab at* VICTOR's *wound.*

ERNEST (*quite quietly*): What a place, eh?

Silence for a moment.

VICTOR: Help me with my shirt, would you?

PETER *helps* VICTOR *with his shirt, ripping it away from the wound.*

ERNEST: It reminds us of the moors of Northumberland.

Silence for a moment.

I love those moors. They're my wife.

VICTOR *has a large hole in his right shoulder, it is covered in blood.*

WILFRED (*watching them*): How is it?

VICTOR: It doesn't look too good.

PETER *is dabbing at the wound with the torn shirt and the rag.*

WILFRED: You go first then. One by one.

Silence for a few moments.

Right?

VICTOR: Yes.

A slight pause.
VICTOR *moves fast, bending low, towards the sunken road.*
A round of enemy rifle-fire rings out.
VICTOR *has gone.*
Silence.

ERNEST: I couldn't ever ask for anything more than those moors like, yer know.

PETER: Or the Pennines, Ernie.

ERNEST *smiles.*

PETER: Out on those moors with a paper kite. Made from the *Daily Sketch*. Newspapers flying like air.

PETER *prepares to run.*

WILFRED: You ready, Peter?

PETER: Yes.

A slight pause.
   PETER *runs. As he does so: sudden blackout.*

Scene Three

The lights are snapped up.
A ward in a convent hospital on the outskirts of Barcelona.
Two beds. A table and a chair. The table has various hospital records and notes on it. Wednesday, March 3rd. Night.
It is impossible to see who the occupants of the beds are: but they are, in fact, VICTOR *and* EDWARD LONGRESSE.
   LUCY ELLISON *is sitting on a chair beside* VICTOR's *bed.*
   SISTER MARY-JOSEPH *is standing beside* EDWARD's *bed. She has a flashlight in her hand.*
   MARY-JOSEPH *was born in 1913. She is a thin, quite tall woman with a brisk, efficient manner. She is wearing the black and white habit of the nursing order, and there are rosary-beads and a crucifix which hang from the belt on her waist.*

MARY-JOSEPH: Why don't you go and get some sleep?

LUCY (*shaking her head*): No.

EDWARD *is on a drain, which runs from the bottom of his lungs, to a bottle on the floor. Occasionally, throughout the scene, a reddish-brown liquid drips down the clear pipe.*
   MARY-JOSEPH *picks up the bottle. It is half-full. She looks at it, and then puts it down. She switches the flashlight on, opens* EDWARD's *eyelids, and shines the flashlight in.*
   VICTOR *stirs. He makes a slight grumbling noise.*
   LUCY *stands up.*

(*Feeling his forehead:*) Victor?

VICTOR *is still.*

He keeps making little grumbling noises.

MARY-JOSEPH: That's only to be expected.

   MARY-JOSEPH *puts the flashlight on the bed. She moves* EDWARD's *covers, finds his wrist, and takes his pulse. She feels his forehead with her other hand.*

LUCY: How is he?

MARY-JOSEPH: Poorly.

LUCY: Has he been shot?

   MARY-JOSEPH *concentrates on her work for a moment.*

MARY-JOSEPH (*putting his wrist back in the bed*): Yes, in the lung, poor devil.

   MARY-JOSEPH *holds the crucifix before her. She prays silently for a moment.*
   She returns to EDWARD, *straightening his bedcovers.*

LUCY: What were you doing, Sister?

MARY-JOSEPH: Praying.

LUCY: For him?

MARY-JOSEPH: And his soul. I shouldn't use the word devil.

   MARY-JOSEPH *picks up the flashlight. She goes to* VICTOR's *bed, opens his eyelids, and shines the flashlight in.*
   The sound of an aeroplane far overhead.
   MARY-JOSEPH *turns the flashlight off and puts it on the bed. She finds* VICTOR's *wrist and takes his pulse. She returns his wrist to the bedcovers. She picks up the flashlight, walks to the table, and sits down.*

LUCY: Aren't you going to take his blood pressure?

MARY-JOSEPH: I don't think I need to anymore.

   MARY-JOSEPH *writes up her hospital notes.*
   A slight pause.
   LUCY *sits down in her chair.*
   A slight pause.

(*Without looking up:*) Why don't you bring your chair over here?

   A slight pause.
   LUCY *picks up her chair. She sits down at the table.*
   MARY-JOSEPH *is still writing.*
   A slight pause.

LUCY: How old are you, Sister?

MARY-JOSEPH: Twenty-four.

LUCY: You seem so old.

   A slight pause.

Am I in your way?

A bomb from the aeroplane explodes in the far distance.
    LUCY's shoulders rise in instinctive fear.

What if one of them should hit us?

A bomb explodes in the far distance.
MARY-JOSEPH has still not looked up from her writing.
A slight pause.
She looks up.

MARY-JOSEPH: How did you find your brother?

LUCY (*frightened*): I was told he was at Jarama, by brigade headquarters. Then I heard they'd been more or less wiped out. No one knew, so I went round the hospitals.

A bomb explodes in the distance.

They're getting nearer.

MARY-JOSEPH (*gently smiling*): You're a remarkable girl.

LUCY: I don't feel it.

MARY-JOSEPH *writes*.

Is war always like this?

A slight pause.

MARY-JOSEPH (*without looking up*): Sleep at the table. I'll let you know if there's any change.

A bomb explodes in the distance.

LUCY: Is the bombing always at night?

A pause.

MARY-JOSEPH (*looking up briefly. Smiling gently*): Notes. I like to do things properly. Your brothers' life may depend on it.

A slight pause.

(*Writing. Not showing her fear:*) It helps me not to think about the bombs.

A bomb explodes in the distance.

They'll go in a minute. This is one raid.

A slight pause.

LUCY: I'm sorry, Sister.

MARY-JOSEPH (*without looking up*): What for?

LUCY: I don't know.

MARY-JOSEPH *leaves her writing. She sits back in her chair.*

Why are you looking at me?

MARY-JOSEPH: What're you doing here?

A bomb explodes in the distance.

LUCY: I came to find my brother.

MARY-JOSEPH *is still looking at her.*
LUCY *feels uncomfortable.*

I love him.

A slight pause.
    MARY-JOSEPH *goes back to writing her notes.*

MARY-JOSEPH: You must really love him, to come all this way.

LUCY: I do. I had to find out for myself.

MARY-JOSEPH: I'm an only child. There was only me.

LUCY (*after a moment's pause*): Why d'you say these things?

MARY-JOSEPH *sits back.*

MARY-JOSEPH: I had to have the faith of absent brothers and sisters. (*Gently smiling:*) My faith is my love.

LUCY *half-smiles.*

Sometimes I –

LUCY (*after a moment's pause*): What?

MARY-JOSEPH (*she doesn't know if she can explain*): You're just a girl.

A slight pause.

Wonder. Sometimes I wonder. I've counted them. Seventy-eight men have died in this hospital in this war. Those that live, go back.

LUCY: They told me I'd be driving an ambulance.

MARY-JOSEPH *writes her notes.*

I do believe in God, Sister, if that's what you're saying.

MARY-JOSEPH: I'm talking about the foolishness of men.

LUCY: Is that why you pray?

MARY-JOSEPH: He's an atheist. A rude one.

LUCY: Who?

LUCY *looks briefly towards* EDWARD's *bed.*

MARY-JOSEPH: I shouldn't talk about the devil, but he makes me. In fun, but he means it.

LUCY (*after a moment's pause*): Where're you from?

MARY-JOSEPH: South London.

LUCY *nods*.

LUCY: I don't know London. I went to the ILP.

MARY-JOSEPH: Haven't you come to fight fascism? That's all they seem to talk about.

LUCY: Err. yes.

MARY-JOSEPH: I don't believe adventure would bring you here.

A slight pause.

LUCY: Why've you come then?

A slight pause.

Sister?

EDWARD (*calling*): Sister?

MARY-JOSEPH *puts down her pen, she goes to him.*

MARY-JOSEPH (*gently*): What is it?

EDWARD (*he has difficulty speaking*): My throat's full of blood. Can I sit up?

MARY-JOSEPH: The drain should be doing that.

EDWARD: It doesn't always work.

EDWARD *sits up.* MARY-JOSEPH *helps him. She props up his pillows.* EDWARD *leans back.*

Thank you, Sister.

MARY-JOSEPH *takes his wrist, she takes his pulse.*

How is it?

MARY-JOSEPH: Ninety to the dozen.

EDWARD: I'm not dead yet then?

MARY-JOSEPH (*gently*): No. Unfortunately.

EDWARD: A pity.

MARY-JOSEPH: Exactly, Mr Longresse.

EDWARD (*coughing*): Sister, has my wife arrived?

MARY-JOSEPH: No, not yet.

EDWARD: She probably can't get through.

MARY-JOSEPH: She will.

EDWARD *coughs*.

How ever do I stop you talking?

EDWARD: You can't.

MARY-JOSEPH *rests his wrist gently on the bed.*

(*Catching his breath*:) Does she know I've moved hospitals?

MARY-JOSEPH (*gently*): We'll tell her. Stop worrying.

EDWARD (*his hand going to her bottom*): You're a pet.

MARY-JOSEPH (*quickly moving out of the way*): Don't you dare. (*Looking at him:*) Try and sleep.

MARY-JOSEPH *returns to the table, she sits down.*

EDWARD (*calling*): Are letters getting through to England?

MARY-JOSEPH: I don't know.

EDWARD: I would like to see her. (*After a moment's pause. Modestly:*) I don't want to put anyone out.

MARY-JOSEPH *is writing.*

(*More quietly:*) This is a bloody war.

A slight pause.

Thank you, Sister.

A handbell rings in the next ward.
MARY-JOSEPH *picks up the flashlight, turns it on, and exits.*

Excuse me. Could you help me?

LUCY *goes to* EDWARD.

I'd like a cigarette. My tobacco's under the mattress.

LUCY *looks where* EDWARD *is showing her. She finds his tobacco, his cigarette papers, and his matches. She gives them to him.*

LUCY: You shouldn't smoke.

EDWARD: Why not?

ACT TWO   47

EDWARD *starts to roll a cigarette. He is well practised.*
VICTOR *stirs very slightly.* LUCY *moves the few feet to his bed, she looks at him.*
VICTOR *is still.*

Where are you from?

LUCY (*moving the few feet back*): Yorkshire.

EDWARD: Oh, yes? I know Yorkshire. My wife and I have tented in the dales.

LUCY: Whereabouts?

EDWARD: At Ripon, I believe.

LUCY: You shouldn't smoke.

EDWARD: This cigarette is between ourselves. It's not for her God-like ears. (*Catching his breath:*) Or nose more precisely. I don't think you're a nurse? You're not behaving like one.

LUCY: No, I came to drive an ambulance.

EDWARD: Good for you. With the ILP?

LUCY: Yes.

EDWARD (*suddenly showing pain*): It's a beastly bloody place, Spain.

LUCY: Can I help?

EDWARD (*covering the pain up*): I miss my wife the most of all.

VICTOR (*stirring slightly. Calling out*): Sister.

LUCY *goes to him.*

LUCY: She's in another ward.

VICTOR: Where am I?

LUCY: Barcelona.

VICTOR *is still and silent.*
A slight pause.
LUCY *moves the few feet back to* EDWARD*'s bed.*

He's my brother. He was brought here from the field hospital at Villarejo de Saluanes. So the Sister said.

VICTOR (*smiling gently*): Don't worry.

EDWARD *licks the cigarette paper.*

LUCY: Where were you injured?

EDWARD: Madrid. (*Catching his breath:*) They can't, or won't, get the bloody bullet out. I'd have a go.

EDWARD *has rolled the cigarette.*
MARY-JOSEPH *enters with the flashlight which is still on.*
EDWARD *quietly hides his cigarette and tobacco.*
MARY-JOSEPH *has gone to* VICTOR. *She opens his eyelids and shines the flashlight in.*
LUCY *watches.*

LUCY: Is he all right?

MARY-JOSEPH (*after a moment's pause*): Mmm. Your brother's pulling through.

MARY-JOSEPH *turns the flashlight off and puts it on the bed. She finds* VICTOR*'s wrist and starts to take his pulse.*

VICTOR (*quietly*): Where am I?

MARY-JOSEPH: Barcelona.

VICTOR: Have I had the operation?

MARY-JOSEPH: Yes, a few hours ago.

EDWARD: Comrade?

MARY-JOSEPH (*snapping at* EDWARD): Quiet.

VICTOR (*trying to remember*): Where am I?

MARY-JOSEPH: In Barcelona. In a convent hospital. (*Putting her hand on his forehead:*) You're much better here. (*Bending down to him:*) Listen, you must sleep.

VICTOR: I feel sick.

MARY-JOSEPH: That's the anaesthetic. (*Almost whispering:*) You're doing very nicely.

VICTOR: You're beautiful, Sister.

MARY-JOSEPH (*smiling*): Sleep, that's the main thing now.

A slight pause.
MARY-JOSEPH *puts* VICTOR*'s wrist back into the bed.*

He mustn't be woken.

LUCY: Yes, Sister.

MARY-JOSEPH *picks up her flashlight and walks to the table.*

EDWARD (*to* LUCY): She's an ogre, that one.

LUCY (*sitting down*): Talking will do you no good.

EDWARD: It's because I'm an atheist, isn't it?

MARY-JOSEPH: If you wish to meet your maker in that condition.

    MARY-JOSEPH *holds the crucifix before her. She prays silently for a moment.*
    LUCY *and* EDWARD *watch her.*
    MARY-JOSEPH *writes her notes.*

EDWARD (*to* LUCY, *but quite loudly*): She doesn't mean it.

MARY-JOSEPH: Don't I, Mr Longresse?

EDWARD: Sister's faith wanders too.

MARY-JOSEPH: I have never been more serious.

EDWARD (*directly to her*): You're not as committed as you seem, Sister.

    EDWARD *coughs. He coughs and coughs.*
    MARY-JOSEPH *takes a small metal bowl from a drawer in the table. She takes it to* EDWARD.
    LUCY *moves out of the way. She watches.*
    MARY-JOSEPH *rubs* EDWARD*'s back, pushing the top of his body gently forward.*

MARY-JOSEPH (*gently*): Careful, careful, careful. Try not to strain the lung.

EDWARD'*s coughing eases.*

That's it.

EDWARD *stops.*

Spit it out.

EDWARD *spits out blood into the bowl.*
VICTOR *stirs very slightly.*

EDWARD: Thank you, Sister.

MARY-JOSEPH: When you feel the coughing starting, try and hold it back.

EDWARD (*catching his breath*): Yes.

MARY-JOSEPH: We want the blood to drain, and not come up.

EDWARD (*catching his breath*): Yes.

MARY-JOSEPH: I'll make sure you see the doctor first in the morning. (*Annoyed with him:*) You do know you're killing yourself, don't you?

EDWARD (*strongly*): No, Sister. I don't care for my own comfort.

A handbell rings.
    MARY-JOSEPH *returns to the table with the metal bowl. She picks up the flashlight, turns it on, and exits to another ward the other way.*
A moment's pause.

LUCY: Why d'you provoke her?

EDWARD: She likes it. (*Pointing to the table:*) Go and get a chair.

LUCY: I shouldn't.

A moment's pause.
    LUCY *goes to the table. She brings back her chair. She puts it down.*
    VICTOR *stirs slightly.*

VICTOR: Have I had the operation?

LUCY (*leaning over him*): A few hours ago.

VICTOR: The surgeon was going to try and take the bullets out.

LUCY: They did.

VICTOR: Where am I?

LUCY: Barcelona.

VICTOR: It's taken weeks to get here.

    EDWARD *has taken his cigarette, tobacco, and matches from beneath the covers. He lights the cigarette.*

LUCY (*turning*): You shouldn't smoke.

VICTOR: Can I have a glass of water?

LUCY: You're not allowed any.

VICTOR: I feel sick.

    EDWARD *is smoking, but very gingerly. He coughs.*

LUCY (*turning*): You shouldn't smoke.

VICTOR (*trying to remember*): Where am I?

LUCY: In a convent hospital, I keep saying.

VICTOR: What day is it?

LUCY: Wednesday.

VICTOR: Lucy?

LUCY: Yes, it's me.

    LUCY *smiles.*

A slight pause.

(*Turning:*) He's closed his eyes again.

    EDWARD *is holding the cigarette, rather than smoking it.*

ACT TWO 49

EDWARD (*smiling*): Don't worry.

LUCY: I can't help it.

EDWARD: Where was your brother shot?

LUCY: In the shoulder. At Jarama.

EDWARD: You're a brave girl.

LUCY: I don't think I'm here really. I think I'm in a dream.

EDWARD (*smiling*): You're here.

A bomb explodes in the far distance.

The English have been good in this illegal war. The French. The Americans.

LUCY: Why did you come?

EDWARD: To fight fascism.

LUCY: That's what everyone says. Are you a socialist?

EDWARD: I'm a writer.

EDWARD *coughs. He is not smoking the cigarette.*

LUCY: I've never met a writer before.

LUCY *sits in the chair.*
The cigarette has gone out. EDWARD *re-lights it with a match.*

EDWARD (*the cigarette in his mouth*): I live in Norfolk, in a tiny village.

He puts the spent match back in the box.

(*Taking the cigarette from his mouth*:) My wife and I run the General Stores.

LUCY (*interested*): Really?

EDWARD (*the cigarette in his hand*): In the mornings, and in the evenings, I do my best to write these terribly bad English novels.

EDWARD *coughs.*

Away from the stink of the London literati. (*Coughing slightly again*:) And the nancy poets.

EDWARD *coughs.*

This bloody lung. (*Giving her the cigarette*:) You'd better put this out for me.

LUCY *takes it. She doesn't know what to do with it.*

On the floor.

LUCY *puts it out with her foot.*

Push the tab under the bed.

LUCY *does so.*

(*His eyes focusing on the future*:) I've written reviews for tuppenny-ha'penny magazines. Defending Kipling. Being attacked by the nancy Left.

EDWARD *looks at* LUCY.

I still want to get my own back on the world.

LUCY (*shyly*): I don't understand.

EDWARD *starts to roll another cigarette.*

EDWARD (*smiling at* LUCY): I'd have liked to have used my hands more. To have been a carpenter, I think. That's why I roll these things. (*A broad smile*:) As well as a great writer.

LUCY *smiles.*

At home we have a smallholding at the back of the Stores. My young son has a pig. I have a goat. My wife, the chickens. I make these little wooden animals, just with a chisel. They're hopelessly inadequate.

EDWARD *smiles.*

I'm sorry, I have the eccentric's habit of always talking about myself.

LUCY (*smiling*): No, I like it.

EDWARD (*smiling*): Why?

LUCY *smiles. She shrugs.*
VICTOR *stirs slightly.*
EDWARD *coughs. The tobacco from the cigarette goes all over the bed.*

Oh, damn.

LUCY *goes to* VICTOR.

VICTOR: What time is it?

LUCY: About two o'clock. It's Lucy.

EDWARD *is trying to pick up the tobacco from the bed and get it back into the paper. He coughs slightly.*

It's Lucy, d'you understand? I'm here.

MARY-JOSEPH *enters. The flashlight is on.*

MARY-JOSEPH: Would you come quickly. I've a patient fallen out of bed.

LUCY: Yes.

MARY-JOSEPH *exits.* LUCY *quickly follows her.*

Silence for a moment.

EDWARD (*talkatively*): Comrade? (*After a moment's pause:*) Comrade?

VICTOR *is still.* EDWARD *lies back with his head on the pillows.*

(*Talking to himself:*) Why am I always next to the sleepy ones?

EDWARD *starts to cough. He coughs and coughs. Little splashes of blood spray out of his mouth.*
After a long while he is still and silent.

(*Gently, quietly:*) Could you help me, Comrade?

A bomb explodes in the far distance. It dies to silence.
Sudden blackout.

Scene Four

The lights are snapped up.
The garden of the convent hospital.
Saturday, March 13th.
The sun is shining.
VICTOR is sitting in a wheelchair under the boughs of a tree. He is wearing pyjamas and a dressing-gown, and there is a blanket over his knees and legs. His right arm is in a sling: in his left hand he is holding a pencil. There is some music manuscript paper on his lap. VICTOR is trying to write.
A slight pause.
MARY-JOSEPH enters, crossing the lawn.

VICTOR (*looking up*): Sister.

MARY-JOSEPH: What is it? I'm busy.

VICTOR: If you're busy, then it doesn't matter.

MARY-JOSEPH *stops.*

MARY-JOSEPH: Yes?

VICTOR: I don't suppose you understand music?

MARY-JOSEPH: Very little. (*Going to him:*) A little.

VICTOR: I'm trying to write down a tune. It's impossible with my left hand. I can't write it quick enough. It's so bloody slow.

MARY-JOSEPH *pulls a face.*

I beg your pardon, Sister.

MARY-JOSEPH: Remind me where we're up to?

VICTOR (*smiling*): This isn't good nursing.

MARY-JOSEPH*'s face hardens.*
They are looking at one another.

MARY-JOSEPH (*severely*): Are you special in any way?

VICTOR: No.

A slight pause.

I had the stitches out this morning, Sister.

MARY-JOSEPH (*softening*): What did the doctor say?

VICTOR: Light exercise.

MARY-JOSEPH: Right then, light exercise it is. Why're you using your left hand?

VICTOR (*hesitating*): Erm – I don't know.

MARY-JOSEPH (*gently*): Take your arm out of the sling.

VICTOR: Yes.

VICTOR *does so.*

I know you have a lot of patients.

MARY-JOSEPH (*kneeling down*): I haven't met a man with more excuses for inactivity.

VICTOR: Have you met any men, Sister.

MARY-JOSEPH (*ignoring that. Gently*): Try and write with it.

VICTOR *puts the pencil in his right hand. He tries to write. His hand is like jelly. The pencil goes all over the place. He stops almost immediately.*

I am not going to sit here unless you're going to try.

VICTOR (*angry*): I am trying, you silly woman.

MARY-JOSEPH: Again.

VICTOR *tries again. The pencil goes all over the place. He looks up.* MARY-JOSEPH *takes his right hand, she helps give strength to* VICTOR*'s wrist.*
VICTOR *manages to write a few notes. He looks up at her.*

It's common sense, isn't it?

VICTOR: My arm feels like jelly, that's all.

ACT TWO   51

MARY-JOSEPH: It will for a few weeks, until you've strength back in it.

MARY-JOSEPH *takes his arm at the elbow and the wrist. By applying pressure, she straightens his arm. It hurts.* VICTOR *pulls a face.*

Tell me when it really hurts.

VICTOR (*quickly*): It really hurts.

MARY-JOSEPH *stops applying the pressure.* VICTOR*'s elbow bends.*
MARY-JOSEPH *applies the pressure, his arm straightens at the elbow.*

(*Pulling a face*:) It really hurts, Sister.

MARY-JOSEPH *stops.*

MARY-JOSEPH: It was a nasty wound. That's good. I've almost got it straight.

MARY-JOSEPH *applies the pressure.* VICTOR *pulls a face.*

VICTOR (*in real pain*): Go on. Go on.

MARY-JOSEPH *has his elbow straight.*

MARY-JOSEPH: I'm going to push your arm up now, so we start to straighten the shoulder.

VICTOR (*wincing*): Will it hurt?

MARY-JOSEPH: Mmm, it might do.

MARY-JOSEPH *keeps* VICTOR*'s arm straight. She moves his arm up so that the shoulder is moved.*

VICTOR (*in real agony*): Might do. Bloody hell.

MARY-JOSEPH: All right?

VICTOR (*gasping*): No.

MARY-JOSEPH *relaxes her pressure,* VICTOR*'s elbow bends, and the arm drops at the shoulder. She keeps hold of his wrist and elbow.*
A slight pause.

MARY-JOSEPH (*gently*): Once more?

VICTOR: No.

MARY-JOSEPH: Well, I'm going to do it.

MARY-JOSEPH *straightens his arm. She moves his arm up so that the shoulder is moved.*
    VICTOR *is in agony. Tears come into his eyes.*
    MARY-JOSEPH *relaxes her pressure. She puts his arm on his lap, and her own hands on her own lap.*
Silence for a moment.

VICTOR (*wiping away the tears with his left hand*): I'm sorry.

MARY-JOSEPH (*gently*): Try using your right hand.

VICTOR *uses his right hand to wipe away the tears. His arm is like jelly, but he succeeds a little bit.*
    VICTOR *is still.*

That's probably enough for an hour or two. We must keep that up.

VICTOR: Why is it so bad?

MARY-JOSEPH: The wound needs time to heal and mend. If we left it without movement, it would just go stiff. You'd lose some mobility in the shoulder.

VICTOR: I haven't to be afraid in other words?

MARY-JOSEPH: That's right.

VICTOR *leans forward, he kisses her on the forehead.* MARY-JOSEPH *pulls her head away.*

I shall pretend you didn't do that. (*After a moment's pause*:) What about this music?

MARY-JOSEPH *takes the manuscript paper and the pencil.*
    VICTOR *looks at her.*

VICTOR: Dorian mode, 3-4. Two crochet rests. A above middle C. A low D. E, F, E, D, G. G, A quavers. B. A minim. A crotchet. Low D. E, F, E, D. A group of six quavers. G. F sharp.

MARY-JOSEPH *looks up from her writing.*

It's a passing note. G. A, B, C. A, dotted minim tied to a minim in the next bar.

VICTOR *sings, quite quietly, a snatch of the tune.*

A, B quavers, C dotted crotchet. B, A, G quavers. A. High D. C, B quavers. A, low D. E, F dotted minim in the next bar. F. G, E quavers. A group of four quavers, D, middle, C, D, E. F, G. C above middle C. B. Low D. E, F quavers. D dotted minim. Double bar line.

MARY-JOSEPH *finishes. She gives him the manuscript paper and the pencil.*

A little music?

MARY-JOSEPH: I learnt at home. My father was a musician.

VICTOR: Why're you so modest?

MARY-JOSEPH (*starting to stand up*): I should be going, I have work to do.

VICTOR (*putting his hand out to stop her*): Don't go.

MARY-JOSEPH *stays kneeling on her haunches.* VICTOR *takes his hand away.*

MARY-JOSEPH (*embarrassed, she is not sure where to look*): This is most irregular.

VICTOR (*realising*): I'm sorry, Sister, you must go.

A slight pause.

I didn't mean to embarrass you.

MARY-JOSEPH *stands up. She is still.*

MARY-JOSEPH (*suddenly giggling*): The Holy Father would wonder what was going on, being kissed by a man.

VICTOR *smiles.*

VICTOR: I shan't do it again, I promise.

MARY-JOSEPH: My Mother Superior might have a fit. I'm a Sister of Mercy, not a Sister of Love.

MARY-JOSEPH *looks as if she is about to burst into tears. She walks away, back to the wards.*

VICTOR: Sister, come back.

MARY-JOSEPH *stops. She has her back to him.*
VICTOR *steps out of the wheelchair. He walks towards her. He stops.*

Listen, I'm sorry, I really am.

A slight pause.

Forgive me?

MARY-JOSEPH: Am I such a foolish young girl that you feel you can do what you want?

(*Turning to face him:*) Sit in your wheelchair, please.

VICTOR (*after a moment's pause*): All right.

VICTOR *walks back to the wheelchair.*

MARY-JOSEPH: Sitting, not standing.

VICTOR *sits in the wheelchair.*
Sudden blackout.

Scene Five

The lights are snapped up.
A small river about two kilometres from the hospital. The river is in a gully which is wooded on either side. A wooden jetty stretches out from the river bank.
Saturday, April 3rd.
The sun is shining brightly through the trees.
MARY-JOSEPH is sitting on the end of the jetty, her feet are above the water. She has taken off her shoes and stockings and they are beside her.
VICTOR is standing at the other end of the jetty, by the bank. He has just entered. He is wearing civilian clothes and he is using his arm almost normally.
VICTOR is looking at her. MARY-JOSEPH is looking at the river, she looks deep in thought.
A pause.

VICTOR: Mary-Joseph.

MARY-JOSEPH (*without turning*): Sister Mary-Joseph. (*Turning to look at him:*) How long've you been there?

VICTOR: Not very long. (*Walking forward:*) They told me at the hospital you'd come along here.

MARY-JOSEPH (*covering her legs*): I'm naked, practically.

VICTOR *sits down beside her. He kisses her on the forehead.* MARY-JOSEPH *kisses his forehead.*

Where've you been these last few days?

VICTOR: Helping Lucy with the ambulance.

MARY-JOSEPH: More casualties?

VICTOR: Yes.

MARY-JOSEPH: It's a real war, isn't it? I thought it would all be over in a few weeks.

VICTOR: I'm going back to the front. I wanted you to be the first to know.

MARY-JOSEPH: Why?

VICTOR: To help us try and win.

MARY-JOSEPH: No, why did you want me to be the first to know?

VICTOR (*smiling*): Because you're my friend.

MARY-JOSEPH: That sounds so simple.

VICTOR: It is.

MARY-JOSEPH *smiles*.

What's the matter?

MARY-JOSEPH: I've had a telling off.

VICTOR: Oh, dear.

MARY-JOSEPH: From the Mother Superior. She was furious. (*Smiling*:) Far worse than my Mother Superior in England, and she could be terrifying.

VICTOR: What about?

MARY-JOSEPH: Don't be silly, Victor. Isn't it obvious to you?

VICTOR: No.

MARY-JOSEPH (*smiling*): It is to her.

VICTOR (*smiling*): Have tongues wagged?

MARY-JOSEPH: Somebody's has.

VICTOR: I'll go and see her. It's not fair that you should have this.

MARY-JOSEPH: You can't just go and see her.

VICTOR: Why not?

MARY-JOSEPH: Well, you can try.

VICTOR: Let me tell her about our friendship. I don't want you in hot water. I like you too much for that.

MARY-JOSEPH *smiles*.

MARY-JOSEPH: It will do no good. They live in worlds of their own, these people. Who knows what they believe, or why.

VICTOR (*gulping*): Goodness.

MARY-JOSEPH: What have I said?

VICTOR: I don't know, Sister. An awful lot, suddenly.

VICTOR *quickly starts to take his shoes off. He uses his right arm carefully.* MARY-JOSEPH *watches him for a moment.*

You're still being careful with that right arm, aren't you?

VICTOR: A little bit.

MARY-JOSEPH: You shouldn't be by now.

VICTOR *rolls his trouser legs up. He jumps off the jetty. He walks out across the shallow water. He stops some distance away.*

VICTOR: What's your real name, Mary-Joseph?

MARY-JOSEPH: That's not a question you ask. Bernadette.

VICTOR: After Bernadette of Lourdes?

MARY-JOSEPH: Yes.

VICTOR: Bernadette what?

MARY-JOSEPH: Bernadette Cook.

VICTOR: Well, Bernadette Cook, what do I say to the Mother Superior?

A slight pause.

MARY-JOSEPH: Don't, Victor, please.

A slight pause.

VICTOR: I'm sorry. (*After a moment's pause*:) I'm finding it hard not to feel the way I do.

MARY-JOSEPH (*she wants to know*): Is that my fault?

VICTOR (*after a moment's pause*): No.

MARY-JOSEPH (*looking at him*): I love you.

A slight pause.

VICTOR: That's both of us in love then.

MARY-JOSEPH (*after a moment's pause*): I'm trying not to.

A slight pause.

Doesn't my faith matter to you?

VICTOR: Yes, it does.

VICTOR *walks back. He climbs onto the jetty. He sits beside her.*

Yes, it does.

MARY-JOSEPH: How much does it matter?

VICTOR: A lot. I can't say. I don't want to see you hurt.

MARY-JOSEPH: I didn't deny it to the Mother Superior.

VICTOR (*brightly*): Mary-Joseph.

A pause.

MARY-JOSEPH: I know what she'll do.

VICTOR: What?

MARY-JOSEPH: Send me somewhere else. Like they sent me here to Spain.

VICTOR *is looking at her.*

I was foolish enough in England to tell the Mother Superior, that I didn't love God as much as I thought I could.

A slight pause.

Isn't that a terrible admission?

VICTOR (*gently*): For you, yes.

MARY-JOSEPH: You know why she sent me?

VICTOR: To defend the church against the Republic.

MARY-JOSEPH: She thought if I saw the churches being burnt –

A slight pause.

I'd think –

A slight pause.

It worked until the war began, and I saw the wounded.

A slight pause.

I still do hate the desecration. But somehow it doesn't seem to matter any more. Because the Church here has nothing to do with the people. (*Almost smiling:*) My Mother Superior would have me in Hell.

A slight pause.

It must be hard for you to understand what I'm saying?

VICTOR: Perhaps, yes.

MARY-JOSEPH: What a sin it is?

A slight pause.

Can you understand?

VICTOR (*carefully*): I think I know what it's like to have a faith, and believe.

MARY-JOSEPH: Honestly?

VICTOR: I didn't, I haven't. You're a part of that understanding. And the war is, too.

MARY-JOSEPH (*smiling*): We're alike.

VICTOR: Mmm.

A slight pause.

MARY-JOSEPH: This doesn't help me decide.

VICTOR (*firmly*): I can't be a part of that decision.

MARY-JOSEPH: That's the most stupid thing you've said.

VICTOR: My life's far too complicated for you.

A slight pause.

MARY-JOSEPH: I wonder if God meant it this way? The simple things are the most truthful.

VICTOR: Have you asked God?

MARY-JOSEPH: Yes.

VICTOR: What did He say?

A slight pause.

MARY-JOSEPH (*looking at him*): I think God can only guide those who are certain.

VICTOR *is looking at her. He looks away.*

If Christ had truly entered my heart –

VICTOR (*after a moment's pause. Still looking down*): Then what?

MARY-JOSEPH: I couldn't love you.

A slight pause.

I am certain. I think finally God has spoken.

A slight pause.

I've no sin in my heart.

VICTOR (*sliding off the jetty, walking away*): You don't know what you're saying.

VICTOR *turns, he looks at her.*

MARY-JOSEPH: God forgives you, Victor.

VICTOR (*shaking his head slightly*): No. No, he doesn't.

MARY-JOSEPH: Yes, he does.

VICTOR: I can't love you. (*Looking at* MARY-JOSEPH:) She was right.

MARY-JOSEPH: Who?

VICTOR (*after a moment's pause*): Elizabeth's Aunt – Edward's Aunt.

MARY-JOSEPH: Who was she?

A slight pause.

VICTOR: It's something that haunts me.

A slight pause.

MARY-JOSEPH: Tell me?

VICTOR (*after a moment's pause*): She said I'd no soul. That I didn't care.

A slight pause.

That I'd no passion. That I'd never cry.

A slight pause.

I did love Edward, in my own way. I think she knew that.

A slight pause.

(*To himself:*) I think so. I think she did know that.

A slight pause.

(*To* MARY-JOSEPH:) I don't know where he is now. I've not seen him for fourteen years.

MARY-JOSEPH: Who?

VICTOR: Edward. He writes novels. He's successful. I'm a bit jealous.

MARY-JOSEPH: Why don't you find him? If he was your friend.

VICTOR: I think I will. (*After a moment's pause:*) He might not want to see me.

MARY-JOSEPH: Why not?

VICTOR (*shrugging*): I don't know.

A slight pause.

(*Shaking:*) I could get in touch with his publisher, maybe. (*Hardly able to get the words out:*) Write to him and explain.

MARY-JOSEPH *slips off the jetty. She goes to him, and stops a short distance away.*

MARY-JOSEPH: You're shaking. Why?

VICTOR (*his whole body shaking*): I don't know.

MARY-JOSEPH: What's the matter?

VICTOR (*the words hardly coming out*): I'm frightened.

MARY-JOSEPH: What of?

VICTOR (*trying to stop it, but he can't*): Letting go.

MARY-JOSEPH: Stop it, Victor.

VICTOR: I can't.

His whole body is shaking.

I can't.

MARY-JOSEPH: What are you frightened of?

VICTOR: I don't know. (*The words hardly coming out:*) Loving you, I think. I'm afraid.

MARY-JOSEPH: Why're you afraid?

VICTOR: I've been running.

MARY-JOSEPH (*puzzled*): Who from?

VICTOR *is still shaking violently.*

VICTOR: I'm sorry.

MARY-JOSEPH: Don't worry.

A slight pause.

Don't worry.

VICTOR *begins slowly, to control himself.*
A pause.
VICTOR *is almost still.*

Is that better?

VICTOR (*the shaking starting again*): This has never happened before.

VICTOR *controls it. He is still.*

A slight pause.

MARY-JOSEPH: I'd like to kiss you, very much.

They move to kiss. Their noses bump.

Whoops.

Sudden blackout.

Scene Six

The lights are snapped up.
The river. The jetty.
A few days later.
The sun is shining brightly through the trees.
The three soldiers are on leave, they are with LUCY. LUCY *is sitting, with her shoes and stockings next to her, on the jetty.*
WILFRED *is sitting close by, he too has his shoes and socks off. They are both writing letters.*

PETER *and* ERNEST *are paddling, some distance apart, in the shallow water. They are still.* PETER *is bending over, looking at something.*
A pause.
ERNEST *walks to* PETER, *he bends over to look.*
PETER: Lots of little fishes.
A pause.
PETER *walks to the jetty. He climbs up. He sits.*
ERNEST *paddles through the water to somewhere else. He bends down, he looks.*
ERNEST: There's a few here as well.
A pause.
Sudden blackout.

Scene Seven

The lights are snapped up. Guisborough, High Cliff. Wednesday, May 26th. Early evening. A red sky which is beginning to darken. A few twinkling lights, from the town down below, can just be seen.
THOMAS ELLISON *is sitting on the grass. He is wearing a shirt and an unbuttoned waistcoat.*
PEGGY SMITH *is standing some distance away. She is wearing a summer coat.*
THOMAS *turns.*
THOMAS: Peggy.
He stands up. PEGGY *walks towards him.*
Have you come to say goodbye?
PEGGY: Yes.
THOMAS *kisses her on the cheek.*
They hesitate for a moment and then both sit on the grass.
(*Smiling:*) I hope I'm all packed and ready.
THOMAS (*starting to take it off*): Here, sit on my waistcoat.
PEGGY: No.
THOMAS (*keeping it on*): Are you sure?
They smile at one another.
What time are you leaving?

PEGGY: We'd like to make as early a start as is possible. Daddy's loading the Riley now.
THOMAS *nods.*
THOMAS: I'm not very good at goodbyes.
CONSTABLE WILLIAM PRICE *enters from the surrounding woods. He is not wearing his uniform, but civilian clothes: trousers, waistcoat and jacket.*
Willy.
PRICE *joins them. He squats down.*
PRICE: I heard someone'd seen a pine marten in the woods. Yer've not seen it by any chance?
THOMAS: No.
PRICE: There's supposed to be a family of 'em. There was a male and female years ago, but they disappeared.
PEGGY: Why was that, Mr Price?
PRICE: I reckon they don't like people much. There's a few rabbits up here. Yer'd've thought they might stay.
PRICE *starts to stand up.*
THOMAS: Yer all right, Willy.
PRICE (*sitting*): I really wanted to see 'em. (*After a moment's pause:*) Yer off tomorrow then?
PEGGY: Yes.
PRICE: Yer still goin' to be doctoring where yer goin?
PEGGY: Yes. I think it's time I let my father get on with his own work, unhindered.
PRICE: Isn't he upset?
PEGGY: He understands why. It's been difficult, at times, living under his shadow.
THOMAS: Wouldn't you do the same, Willy?
PRICE: I'm not that clever.
PRICE *stands up.*
My supper will be on the table.
PEGGY (*looking up at him*): I thought you were treated very shoddily.
PRICE: A few folk've said that.
PEGGY: I'm sorry.

PRICE: It's one of those things. All the best.

PEGGY *stands up.*

See yer, Thomas.

THOMAS: No doubt.

PRICE *exits the way he came.*

PEGGY: He was treated very shabbily. Wasn't he?

THOMAS: I don't know. Yes, probably.

PEGGY *sits.*

I don't feel sorry for him. He should have done something about it. It wasn't just generosity. He wanted a quiet life. He was bound to be sacked sooner or later. The world is changing.

PEGGY *smiles.*

Shouldn't you be seeing Dorothy?

PEGGY: Yes, at eight o'clock. Is that why you came up here?

THOMAS (*smiling*): I said I hate goodbyes. (*After a moment's pause:*) She's upset.

PEGGY: I'm not sure how to handle her?

THOMAS: I wouldn't. Be yourself. She'll get over it. (*After a moment's pause:*) I know she's been grateful to you.

PEGGY: It's mutual. I've enjoyed her company.

THOMAS: I don't know if she knows why you have to go.

PEGGY *looks down.*

PEGGY (*looking back up*): Do you?

THOMAS: I think so, Peggy.

PEGGY: When did you find out?

THOMAS: A second ago. I've had my doubts for months.

A slight pause.

I shan't ever tell her. I don't know what will become of Victor. It almost seems irrelevant, in a way.

PEGGY: I'm guilty of breaking their marriage.

THOMAS: Perhaps.

PEGGY: I loved him, you know.

A slight pause.

THOMAS: Thank you.

PEGGY (*she doesn't understand*): Why?

THOMAS: Because there is nothing to be gained from saying anything else. Dorothy will give her own thanks.

A slight pause.

It's a long way, isn't it?

PEGGY (*firmly*): Yes.

THOMAS: If you ever come back, come and see us.

PEGGY: Who can say?

An aeroplane circles far overhead.

I would be happier, if you didn't tell Dorothy.

THOMAS: I've said I shan't.

PEGGY: Were you hiding up here?

THOMAS: No. If I saw you I would have to say something.

A slight pause.

I didn't want to upset you. I was hiding. But for the right reasons.

A slight pause.

PEGGY: I hope I'm doing the right thing. I told my father. He was furious. I felt I owed him an explanation.

A slight pause.

I would be happier if Dorothy didn't know.

THOMAS: Stop yourself from saying anything, Peggy.

PEGGY: I will, I'll try.

THOMAS (*after a moment's pause*): The truth is often right. In this case, it isn't.

The aeroplane goes.

In any case, it's not that far.

PEGGY: Where?

THOMAS: To Canada. We'll come and see you.

PEGGY *smiles, half-laughs.*
It won't be that far in a few years' time. The world is getting smaller.

PEGGY: It seems a long way to me.

THOMAS: Why did you love him Peggy?

PEGGY: Didn't you?

THOMAS: Yes, I did.

PEGGY: Then you know why.

THOMAS: No, I don't.

A slight pause.

He's one of the most selfish people I've ever met.

A slight pause.

The world is changing, isn't it?

A slight pause.

It's not me. Or even Victor. Or you. It's something in the air. (*After a moment's pause:*) War, perhaps. (*After a moment's pause:*) It's almost as if we're getting ready. The world will turn again. Thank God, I'll be too old this time.

THOMAS *smiles.*

PEGGY: What're you smiling for?

THOMAS: Because I'm helpless. (*He stands up quickly.*) Perhaps I do understand why Victor went to Spain.

PEGGY *flinches for a split second, feeling for a moment that* THOMAS *might hit her.*

Ask Dorothy to show you Lucy's letter.

PEGGY: How is Lucy?

THOMAS: Her letters are full of her brother. He's back at the front, apparently. Or will be by now, fighting. She's a Spanish boyfriend.

PEGGY: I'd rather not see it. I've tried not to show any interest.

A slight pause.

THOMAS: You sail from Southampton?

PEGGY: Yes. On Saturday morning. (*After a moment's pause:*) My father's still taking me.

A slight pause.

Do you think I'm doing the right thing?

THOMAS: I hope so, Peggy, for your sake

PEGGY: My father didn't want me to go. Now, he can't wait. Isn't that awful?

THOMAS: No.

PEGGY: Is being in love such a sin?

THOMAS (*after a moment's pause*): Yes.

A slight pause.

We're all going to have to change. Aren't we?

PEGGY (*running her hands through her hair*): I'm sorry, I feel faint.

PEGGY *sits with her head between her knees.*

THOMAS: Don't worry.

A slight pause.

PEGGY (*sitting up*): That's better. It's gone.

PEGGY *smiles.*

THOMAS: What time does your boat sail on Saturday morning?

PEGGY: Eight o'clock.

Sudden blackout.

Scene Eight

The lights are snapped up.
The wooded coppice at ELIZABETH BRADLEY's *house by the river Thames in Twickenham.*
The summer of 1946.
A bright sunlight is filtering through the apple trees.
There is a lawnmower, turned upside-down, on the grass. The green hopper is elsewhere on the lawn.
ELIZABETH BRADLEY *is kneeling beside the lawnmower. She is wearing trousers and a cardigan. There is a hammer and a small oilcan beside her: she is tampering, very unpractically, at the lawnmower with a wooden-handled screwdriver.*
VICTOR, *wearing trousers and a short-sleeved jumper, is standing some distance away. He has just entered.*
A slight pause.

VICTOR: Elizabeth.

ELIZABETH *turns her head.*
There is a slight pause while she works out who it is.

ELIZABETH (*as if he had never been away. Standing up*): Victor, my dear, how lovely to see you.

ELIZABETH *has the screwdriver in her hand. They are looking at one another.*

VICTOR: It's been a long time.

ELIZABETH: Oh, surely not that long. (*Kicking the lawnmower:*) Now then, dear, whilst you are here, would you fix this thing for me?

VICTOR (*walking forward*): What's the matter with it?

ELIZABETH: Oh, it doesn't work, the usual story. (*Holding up the screwdriver:*) This might not be the right tool.

VICTOR *takes the screwdriver, he bends down, he looks at the lawnmower.*

The things that go round have stopped going round. It's a most nuisant thing.

VICTOR: I'm not very practical.

ELIZABETH: Dear, none of us are. We're all making do.

ELIZABETH *bends down to show him.*

I think it might be somewhere in these little screws.

ELIZABETH *picks up the hammer.*

VICTOR: I wouldn't bash it.

ELIZABETH *kneels down. She bashes at the lawnmower with the hammer.*

ELIZABETH: Is that doing it?

VICTOR (*trying to turn the blades, they still won't move*): No.

ELIZABETH *bashes again.*

(*The screwdriver stuck in the blades:*) No.

ELIZABETH *sits back.*

The house is full of children?

ELIZABETH: Yes, dear. They all paint and sing. (*Standing up, walking away:*) They're all mentally retarded, so they do it very badly. (*Turning to face him:*) I laugh. Quite a lot.

VICTOR (*standing up*): Whose idea was that?

ELIZABETH: Oh, they needed somewhere to express themselves.

VICTOR: It was a shock.

ELIZABETH: Dear, you're so normal.

VICTOR: How many are there?

ELIZABETH: Fifteen. We put on a concert last year. I laughed (*Turning, walking away a pace:*) No, it was something we did in the war, when the bombs were falling. (*Turning to face him:*) How mean the world has become, Victor.

VICTOR (*after a moment's pause*): I came to say various things.

ELIZABETH (*turning, walking away*): I saw Edward the other day. He said you'd met.

VICTOR (*surprised*): Really?

ELIZABETH *is standing with her back to him.*

I thought Edward had died in the Spanish Civil War.

ELIZABETH (*turning*): No, dear, you've got it quite wrong. When I saw your name in my newspaper the other day, I said to Mrs Wellbeloved, that at last you were both successful. Of course Edward has a brilliant streak, dear.

VICTOR (*after a moment's pause*): I'm sorry, Elizabeth. We were in the same hospital. I never knew.

ELIZABETH (*turning, walking away*): He has that touch of genius that you'll always lack.

ELIZABETH *stands with her back to him.*

VICTOR: I came to ask if you'd like to come?

ELIZABETH: No, dear, the children are enough.

A slight pause.

I wondered if I'd upset you that day. The day I offered you money.

VICTOR: No.

A slight pause.

ELIZABETH: I'd hate your music if it wasn't perfect. Has it your soul in it, Victor?

VICTOR: I don't know.

ELIZABETH: Is it mean?

VICTOR: I hope not.

ELIZABETH (*turning to face him*): Don't

you find the world so bloody mean these days? No passion? No commitment? No imagination.

BERNADETTE COOK (SISTER MARY-JOSEPH) *enters. She is wearing a summer dress.*

It's all so bloody small-minded.

BERNADETTE *walks to* VICTOR.

And what do you do, dear?

BERNADETTE: I'm a nurse.

VICTOR *takes her hand.*

One of the children is asking for you.

ELIZABETH: Isn't there a teacher with them?

BERNADETTE: Yes.

ELIZABETH: I'm just the gardener.

VICTOR (*after a moment's pause*): Bernadette nursed Edward.

ELIZABETH (*turning her back on them*): I don't want to know.

VICTOR *and* BERNADETTE *look at one another.* VICTOR *shrugs.*
ELIZABETH *turns to them.*

He died fighting for what he believed in?

VICTOR: Don't you know that already, Elizabeth?

A slight pause.

ELIZABETH: I forget, the war has changed everything. Good, I'm glad.

A slight pause.

How long has it been, Victor?

VICTOR: Twenty-three years. Won't you come to the concert? I thought you might be pleased.

ELIZABETH: I am, dear, I am. No, I saw your name in my newspaper. (*Walking to the lawnmower*:) The world today is full of such horrible things, I only ever read the nice.

ELIZABETH *kneels down. She picks up the can of oil and starts to oil the lawnmower. She bashes at it with the hammer.*
The lights fade.
Darkness.
The company re-sing the opening song. It is symphonic in tone. It is VICTOR*'s.*
As they sing the light grows in intensity.
The end.

Music for the Play

OPENING SONG: THE SLEEPERS

Hard fac-es of an-ger and white eyes of doubt,
She with her palm on the hip of her spouse,
The bo-dies on the battle-field, the in-sane in their rooms, and so the
new-born e-merge from the gates of the old.

CAROL: 'WHILE SHEPHERDS WATCHED'

TUNE: 'Lord Byron' Trad. Words: Martin Carthy

1. Loud we mourned him a-last we bore him our young Bri- / -gadier when we found him, In the ground we gently laid him we beat our drum then we mourned no more. In his mouth there was music ringing at Cerro Rojo with the bullets ringing round him, Come the Stuka from heaven singing muffle your drum for my love sings no more.

2. On my bed where I lay weeping, on my bed there is no resting, Many nights now without sleeping, Thoughts of my love go tumbling round. Dream I see him see him coming. In the clouds I see him standing, Jimmy with the angels round him, Jimmy there in his bloody shroud.

THE SLEEPERS: FINAL CHORUS

Moderato

Lyrics: Hard faces of anger and white eyes of doubt,

Lyrics:
She with her palm on the hip of her spouse

The bodies on the battlefield, insane in their rooms,

And so the new-born emerge from the gates of the old.

(Child's voice) p. As peo-ple lay brea-thing in cur-Ling re- pose,
CHORUS word less
pp
pp
3
p
7
(Child) An o- pen eye Loo-king at those of the closed,
3
7

(Child) pau-sing and ga-zing and ben-ding con-fused,

(Child) And so the new-born e-merge from the gates of the old.

Hands are spread forth from the Lo-vers of doubt

He with his hands on the hip of his spouse.

Swift-ly from sight is borne the brave corpse, and so the

new born e- merge from the gates of the old